The Responsive Chord

The
Responsive Chord

TONY SCHWARTZ

Anchor Press/Doubleday
Garden City, New York

ISBN: 0-385-08893-0
Library of Congress Catalog Card Number 73–81420

To my parents,
my wife, Reenah,
and my children, Kayla and Anton.

Acknowledgments

I wish to thank and acknowledge John Carey's significant contribution to this book. I regard him as a co-author of portions of it.

I wish to thank Ted Carpenter, Joe Napolitan, Art Pearson, Michael Rowan, and Reenah Schwartz for their thoughtful suggestions and criticism in relation to earlier versions of this manuscript.

I want to extend a special thanks to Bill Whitehead of Doubleday for his superb job in editing this book, and for the skillful way he handled our work relationship.

I also wish to thank the Polaroid Corporation for supplying equipment and materials used in researching and illustrating this book.

Contents

Radio and I grew up together, and my ear developed a sensitivity to audio communication, which carried over to other areas of my life. I couldn't read, work, or do homework without the radio on. My mother often complained that people could not read and listen at the same time. She was half right. Some people, those who shared her sensory orchestration, could not attend a strong visual message and a distinct auditory message occurring simultaneously in their environment. But radio reshuffled the interrelations among the senses for those of us who grew up with it, and for generations that followed. I examined my own listening and reading habits very carefully, and noticed that I was oscillating in my reception of auditory and visual stimuli. At one moment I would attend a visual cue (e.g., a word on a page), and in the next instant, attend the auditory stimuli emanating from the radio. Although I was not simultaneously *perceiving* two sensory inputs, the oscillation process was so quick that I could readily absorb distinct auditory and visual information *occurring* simultaneously. This discovery encouraged me to look deeper into the new communication environment.

My first exploration in sound communication was through amateur radio. It was short-lived, however, because I quickly discovered that most "hams" were interested in the technical aspects of the transmission system, not communication from people to people. When I spoke to someone in Africa, Texas, or Australia, they would ask about the equipment I was using or the quality of the signal being received. I would ask about the work they did, the food they ate, the local folk songs, and generally, what life was like in their part of the world. We were not on the same social frequency, and my interest in amateur radio faded after a year or two.

In 1945 I bought a Webster wire recorder, and my life immediately took a new direction. At first I recorded music off the air, particularly those forms of music that did not exist on record—jazz and folk songs. I also developed an acquaintance with many of the great but poor folk performers of the day, such as Josh White, Harry Belafonte, Yma Sumac, Pete Seeger, Moondog, and many others. Most of these performers could not afford a sound mirror (as recorders were called in those days) to hear themselves. I would call performers, after hearing them on the air, and ask if they would like to be recorded. Most of them welcomed the idea because it enabled them to refine their performance and develop new material. The experience taught me a great deal about folklore, the relation between speech and songs in a community, and the function of music in different cultures. It also generated the idea of exchanging recordings with people all over the world. So in 1946 I started the first audio exchange of wire and tape recordings by mail. I placed ads in foreign newspapers offering to send a recording to anyone who would mail a wire or tape of their local music to me. Using this method, I exchanged recordings with over eight hundred people in fifty-two countries, and accumulated some twenty thousand songs and stories.

In 1946 I also began a weekly morning program on the New

York City radio station, WNYC. A wealthy New Yorker who listened to my programs called and asked if he and his wife could visit me. They were very excited by my work and suggested that I leave my job and devote full time to a project in sound. They offered to pay me more than I was currently making, and gave me complete freedom in choosing the project. I quit my job the next day and spent a year and a half studying the sound of life in my postal zone, New York 19. I felt that since I was asking other people to send me the sound and song of their towns and cities, the material would take on greater meaning if I made an in-depth study of the auditory environment in my own neighborhood.

The New York 19 project was to be a documentation of sounds and songs in their *natural* environment. So I did not want to bring a vegetable vendor or street musician into my studio in order to record him. But in 1946 there were no portable recorders. If a sound could not be brought into the studio, a sound effect was created to substitute for reality. I developed a portable recorder specifically for the New York 19 project. It was battery-operated, could be used while walking or running, and weighed about fourteen pounds. Once I was free of Mr. Edison's cables, I could explore the beauty of language in everyday situations and the sounds of life around us.

Moe Asch of Folkways Records heard of my work and asked if I would create some records of sound in everyday life. I conceived and executed a number of records for him, among them, *N.Y. 19; 1,2,3, and a Zing, Zing, Zing; Millions of Musicians; The World in My Mail Box; Music in the Streets; Sounds of My City; Nueva York;* and *The Sound of Children.* I believe these were the first records to capture sound that was part of everyday city life. My material enabled a listener to experience actual sounds—sounds that served vital communicative functions in people's lives.

In the mid-fifties, some people in the advertising world asked me to work on sound in commercials. Among them was

Steve Frankfurt, at that time an up-and-coming art director at
Young & Rubicam. I produced the soundtracks for several Johnson & Johnson baby powder commercials. They were extremely
successful, for a simple reason. I applied the same philosophy
to my commercial work that I had used in my sound docu-
mentaries. It may seem rather obvious now, but the Johnson
& Johnson commercials called for "children's voices," and I
used real children. Previously, all children and baby sounds
had been created by mature women imitating children. I realized that if one could create a sensation in the advertising
world by using real children to create the sound of children's
voices, the industry must be extraordinarily ignorant of how
sound functions in people's lives. It was. I soon found myself
doing a great amount of work for all the major agencies. To
date, I have created over four thousand TV and radio commercials.

Advertising agencies attempted to label my early commercials with numerous deadly compliments. First, I was a "great
specialist in children's sound," then a "sound effects genius."
None of these labels had anything to do with my work. Advertisers, to this day, look perplexed when I tell them I have no
interest in *sound effects*. I am solely interested in the *effect of
sound* on people.

In the early sixties I discovered the work of Marshall
McLuhan. The pop culture that developed around McLuhan,
and the *guru* status accorded him for a while has, unfortunately, clouded the extraordinary contribution he has made to
communication theory. McLuhan's argument that people can
approach a medium from totally different sensory bases allowed me to focus clearly on how I had been working all
along. I realized that I approached sound from an auditory
base, while the rest of the advertising industry was structuring
sound communication from a written, print base.

My association with McLuhan and Ted Carpenter led me
to investigate how auditory communication interacts with the
total communication structure. I knew that the sound environ-

ment documented in my early records had changed radically, and I wanted to discover how mass-mediated sound functions in people's lives today.

In 1967, another dimension was added to my career when I met Joe Napolitan, a political campaign consultant and public affairs analyst. Since then, I have created several thousand radio and TV spots for political campaigns. Joe can precisely and accurately conceptualize communication problems better than anyone I know. Equally important, he creates a work environment within a campaign that permits a communicator such as myself to deal exclusively with the communication problem. This is a crucial element in the *task-oriented approach* to communication discussed later in this book. In addition, Joe is a brilliant researcher, and he has contributed immeasurably to knowledge about reaching and affecting specific audiences.

The knowledge I acquired through knowing Napolitan and McLuhan, along with the findings that emerged from a National Endowment for the Arts study and my years of work in sound, provided the basis for this book.

The Responsive Chord

It is difficult to imagine a person who watched Jack Ruby shoot Lee Harvey Oswald before live television cameras, turning to his wife or children and commenting, "That was an extraordinary *message* we just received." Yet someone analyzing Oswald's televised assassination, from a communication point of view, will be encumbered by such terms as senders, receivers, channels, and messages. In talking about communication, especially mass-media communication, we often find ourselves using terms or analytical models that distort or oversimplify the process. The vocabulary of communication theory consistently fails as a tool for analyzing the mass-media process.

It is not just that we lack adequate terms for describing communication. Our understanding of the communication process is hindered by deep-rooted perceptual and cognitive biases. We believe that communication takes place across large spaces, over a period of time, and primarily through one symbolic mode (words). Though the exchange of verbal messages (typically, written messages) constitutes only a small percentage of human communication, we generalize this one mode as the basis on which all communication is structured. This bias is founded, in part, on Western society's problems in communicating during the five-hundred-year period prior to the development of electronic media, when print was the dominant means of non-face-to-face communication. The movement or transportation of messages across considerable distances in the briefest period of time was the central and overriding communication problem. Most of our communication theories today are still structured around this issue.

TRANSPORTATION THEORIES OF COMMUNICATION

A classic transportation model of the communication process first discusses the source of communication, or the sender. A sender experiences and formulates "meaning" through his encounters with other people and objects in his world. He codes this meaning into a symbolic form—typically, words. He is now ready to send a message, but first he must choose a way of packaging his message for the trip. Writing words on paper could serve as the package, or transmitter, in such a model. Next the sender chooses a channel of communication, such as a letter, newspaper, pamphlet, or book. A channel of communication is often low in efficiency. It requires time to move information across a given space. It may also introduce noise into the message. Newspapers can be censored; pamphlets are written in various *styles*, and this may alter

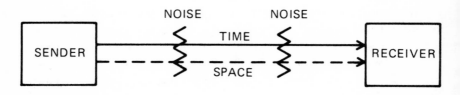

TRANSPORTATION MODEL OF COMMUNICATION

the meaning a sender intended to put into his words; and letters may be damaged in transit.

At the other end of a communication channel is a receiver. He must decode the symbolic forms in the message, assess the damage produced by noise in the channel, and match the "meanings" in the message against his understanding of the world, in order to comprehend the meaning intended by the sender. Communication may be said to take place when the two "meanings" are alike, or to the extent that they match.

The transportation model is not without value. It is a useful guide in analyzing some forms of communication in our society, and it is a good model for illustrating the communication problems in Western society during the print era. Before electricity, the available channels of communication, such as drums, smoke signals, reflecting mirrors, cannon shots, and lantern signals, were subject to severe limitations in the physical environment. Cloudy weather, darkness, trees, and mountains interfered with vision. Animal sounds, wind, thunder, canyons, etc., interfered with auditory signals. Messages had to be formulated according to a rigidly precise code and were limited to only the most crucial data—owing to the inefficiency of the transportation channel. "Getting the message across" was the consummate problem. A military leader who wanted to signal his allies through a system of pennants by day or torches by night had to concern himself with rain or wind extinguishing a torch or blowing over a pennant, and thereby communicating the wrong battle instructions. The problem was compounded when a message was to be sent over a long distance. Napolean established a network of 224 line-of-sight semaphore stations, spanning over 1,000 miles. The coded message had to be repeated accurately at each station for a correct message to get through. The chance of an error was quite high. In addition, these vehicles for transporting messages were single-channel systems. They lacked the multichannel reinforcement of most face-to-face interactions (i.e., in face-to-face encounters we see and hear a person simultaneously; both channels are likely to support the meaning he intends to communicate).

As Western culture developed more complex economic and social structures, the quick and accurate movement of information became more critical. Wars were often prolonged, and sometimes initiated, because of a breakdown in the transportation of messages. Similarly, fortunes were made and lost when one party gained a slight advantage in the time required to send and receive messages across an ocean or continent. An English merchant who discovered that the cotton crop in America was highly successful could undercut his competitors if he alone possessed this information.

As a result of these transportation problems, we came to understand communication as the movement of information across space, over a period of time. We generalized the problem area of communication as synonymous with the process itself. A transportation theory of communication is useful when the *movement* of information is a central problem, but such issues are only a small area in the total communication process.

When someone is overloaded with information, the transportation theory ceases to be meaningful. In addition, transportation theory looks at communication from a "message" point of view. It asks: How are messages created? How do they move? How are they received? Most human communication, however, involves the exchange of so much information at any moment that it cannot be isolated as message units. The transportation theory is thus inadequate in describing the human learning process, or accounting for the dissemination and flow of information in our society. Information flow is a much more complex process than the mere transportation of messages.

The transportation theory of communication is the basis of many formal models of communication as well as our everyday conception of "sending messages." The way we use a postal service to send a letter comes very close to our commonplace analogy for all communication. We assume that communication is difficult to achieve, and that a message encounters resistance at each step along the way. This commonplace conception of communication is so basic to our thinking that we have used the new electronic media almost exclusively as message-sending devices. In my childhood, for example, the telephone was used as a surrogate for a telegram or letter, not as a new medium. If our family was planning to visit relatives in New Jersey, my mother would call long distance from New York to New Jersey to tell them when we expected to arrive. Her messages were short, loudly spoken, and to the point. She used the phone as a vehicle for sending a message across a space. Even when the line between New York and New Jersey was clear, she spoke louder than necessary—conscious of the space between them and using the phone as if it were a tunnel through a chasm. She believed that the phone, like a letter, was a low-efficiency vehicle for communicating, and she was pushing to get her message across. Today, my daughter often calls her friends to exchange giggles. They relate bits of news,

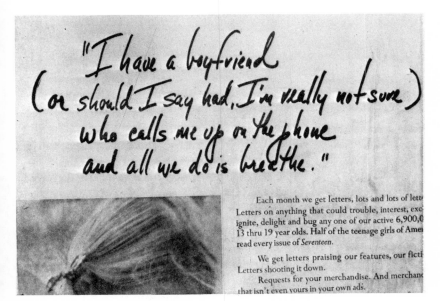

"I have a boyfriend
(or should I say had, I'm really not sure)
who calls me up on the phone
and all we do is breathe."

Each month we get letters, lots and lots of lett Letters on anything that could trouble, interest, exc ignite, delight and bug any one of our active 6,900,0 13 thru 19 year olds. Half of the teenage girls of Amei read every issue of *Seventeen*.

We get letters praising our features, our ficti Letters shooting it down.

Requests for your merchandise. And merchanc that isn't even yours in your own ads.

Part of an ad for Seventeen *magazine.*

giggle back and forth a few minutes, then say goodbye. My daughter accepts the telephone as a communication system with no resistance and no transformation. Communication for her is what happens when you use a telephone, not something that may occur if your message gets through.

Our misconception of communication as transportation interacts with another deep-rooted bias: the identification of print with "meaning." Only a tiny fraction of all communication takes place through print (the U.S. national average for book purchases is .3 book per year, and this represents an all-time high in Western culture), yet it remains an idealized form of communicating the most important information: "I'll believe that when I see it in writing." More significant, print has helped foster a narrow conception of communication that accepts perceptual information as meaningful only to the extent that it conforms to the patterning inherent in print communication. One cannot approach a viable theory of communication until he exorcises the "spirit of print" that has controlled our terms for learning, understanding, and communicating.

THE END OF THE LINE

Print has dominated our non-face-to-face communications environment for the past five hundred years. During this period, the information most valued by Western societies was communicated in a fixed form, with words following one after another, left to right, on lines that proceeded down a page. All preserved knowledge, as well as those pieces of information that achieved high status throughout the society (e.g., laws) were recorded in print. The linear process, by which information was translated into print, took on a status unto itself. As a result, the linear process came to be valued in many areas of people's lives. Our language, for example, shows a marked dependence on linearity in the terms we use for clear thinking and proper behavior. A child growing up in our culture is taught to "toe the line . . . keep in line . . . walk the straight and narrow . . . don't make waves." Similarly, he is told that a good student is one who "follows a clear line of thought." And if someone really understands another person, we say he can "read him like a book." Our logic has been the logic of print, where one idea follows another. "Circular reasoning" is synonymous with unacceptable logic. And we know that you never accomplish anything by "running around in circles."

The linearity in our language is accompanied by a strong dependence on visual analogies to represent truth, knowledge, and understanding. Do you *see* what I mean? A really bright person—i.e. someone with hindsight, foresight, and insight—will see eye to eye with me. But a dull person, one who hasn't seen the light, won't agree with my point of view. Why, it's as clear as ABC.

If seeing was believing, listening and speaking were undependable elements in the communication process. It was a common view that children should be seen and not heard. If you played it by ear, you were not very sure of yourself. And to be recognized as a trained musician, you had to be able to read a score and write notes on paper. In the courtroom, unreliable evidence, whether of a written or spoken variety, may be discarded on the grounds that it is "hearsay." Similarly, a scholar could look back on history, and prophet could see into the future; but if someone crudely imitated another performer, we said he was a weak echo or that he was mouthing something that had been done better. Even the early radio operators indicated that they were receiving a strong signal by saying, "Read you loud and clear."

Even after we recognize the predominance of linear analogies in our language, it becomes important only when we understand that many non-linear patterns in our present communication structure are described and analyzed as linear patterns. Our linear bias also prevents us from understanding preliterate auditory cultures. Few readers of the passage in

Genesis, "In the beginning was the Word," recognize that it refers to a spoken word. Jesus said, "It is written but I say unto you" to assert a new world order based on his spoken words. Linearity and a strong visual orientation are not endemic to all cultures. A society that depends on auditory communication for the exchange of messages will organize their "world" in a very different way from our own. Space, time, the concept of self, etc., take on very different meanings when auditory patterns replace a linear, visual orientation.

You have noticed that everything an Indian does is in a circle, and that is because the Power of the World always works in circles, and everything tries to be round. In the old days when we were a strong and happy people, all our power came to us from the sacred hoop of the nation and so long as the hoop was unbroken the people flourished. . . . Everything the Power of the World does is done in a circle. The Sky is round and I have heard that the earth is round like a ball and so are all the stars. The Wind, in its greatest power, whirls. Birds make their nests in circles, for theirs is the same religion as ours. The sun comes forth and goes down again in a circle. The moon does the same, and both are round.

Even the seasons form a great circle in their changing, and always come back again to where they were. The life of a man is a circle from childhood to childhood and so it is in everything where power moves. Our tipis were round like the nests of birds and these were always set in a circle, the nation's hoop, a nest of many nests where the Great Spirit meant for us to hatch our children.

Hehaka Sapa (Black Elk)
(quoted from *Touch the Earth*, T. C. McLuhan)
Outerbridge & Dienstfrey
New York, 1971, p. 42

In many ways, we are today experiencing a return to an auditory-based communications environment. However, lacking the terms to describe this shift, as well as a perceptual orientation to recognize it, we often fail to understand what is happening. If one keeps his ears to the wall, he will begin to hear this new base echoed in the language of the young. Here, people in agreement are "on the same wavelength" or "on the same frequency." A person learns by "getting around." Some-one who "plays it by ear" is open to new possibilities that may emerge in a situation. Truth is conveyed by "telling it like it is." An individual who learns how to behave properly in a sit-uation "tunes in on what's happening." And effective com-munication "strikes a responsive chord."

Our social organization clearly reflects the shift from a pre-dominantly linear to an acoustic base in communication struc-ture. Lines are disintegrating all around us. The NBC "Today" show has a one-handed clock that indicates minutes past the hour. Since the program is viewed simultaneously in different time zones, it makes sense to tell the audience, "It's ten min-utes past the hour" and assume that they know which hour,

rather than to state, "It's ten past eight in the Eastern Standard zone, ten past seven in the Central Standard zone," etc. This sharing of information across time zones demonstrates how time *lines* have lost significance. Indeed, two western states have petitioned to change their time zone because they receive most television programming from stations in border states with a different time zone. Also, Congress is considering a redistricting of congressional zones to match media districts. Similarly, instantaneous information has reduced the need for datelines in newspapers. One of the cornerstone assumptions in the transportation theory of communication—that a period of time is required for information to move across space—has been undermined by the near-instantaneous speed of electronic communication.

The line, as a means of social organization, is being replaced by acoustic space principles. The "Party line" no longer ex-

plains patterns of voting behavior. The railroad line no longer explains transportation patterns in our society. Even the lines or rows that organized seating patterns in schools, churches, and theaters are giving way to new patterns. Theater-in-the-round has returned. Conference tables and classroom desks are organized in circular patterns. And recently, the governor of a large eastern state defined his role as "Trying to *tune* government to the needs of citizens."

THE AUDITORY BASE OF ELECTRONIC MEDIA

Television and film, as well as radio, tapes, and records, have contributed to a radical transformation in our perception of the world—from a visual, print base to an auditory base. Each of these media conditions the brain to receive and process all

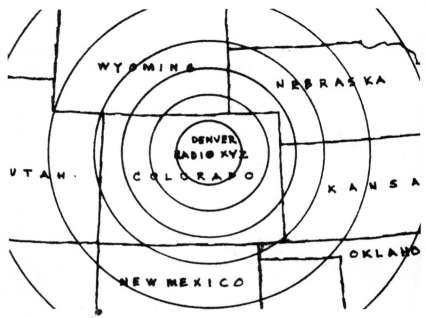

The dispersal pattern of a radio signal is circular. Thus while we pay taxes and vote within the irregular boundaries of city and state lines, we are united to those who share electronically mediated information with us by a circular pattern, the limits of the radio station's audience. This experience has fostered a sense of community that resembles the days before print, when the circular dispersal pattern of a person's voice, or drums, determined social patterns of interaction.

information in the same way it has always processed information received via the ear. The ear receives fleeting momentary vibrations, translates these bits of information into electronic nerve impulses, and sends them to the brain. The brain "hears" by registering the current vibration, recalling the previous vibrations, and expecting future ones. We never hear the *continuum* of sound we label as a word, sentence, or paragraph. The continuum never exists at any single moment in time. Rather, we piece bits of information (millisecond vibrations) together and perceive the entire three-stage process as "hear-ing."

As a wider range of new material reached the public through telephone, radio, film, records, and television, we developed a stronger orientation toward the auditory mode of receiving and processing information. A greater percentage of the information that affected our lives was reaching us in auditory form. This was true not only for sound, but also for electronically mediated visual information, which is patterned like auditory information. Man had never before experienced a world of visual sensation patterned in an auditory mode.

Film transmits visual information by projecting a series of still pictures in rapid succession. Each still frame is projected

In auditory-based cultures, the flow of information is analogous to the dispersal pattern created by dropping a pebble in a bucket of water.

for approximately one fiftieth to one seventy-fifth of a second. Following each frame, the screen is black for a nearly equal length of time. The same frame may then be projected a second time, or the next frame may be shown—depending on the projector. But in any one-second period, the screen is black approximately half the time. The brain "sees" motion by registering the current still picture, recalling previous frames, and anticipating future frames that will complete the movements. This differs considerably from visual experience in everyday life, where the eye is bombarded with a continuous stream of information, which is always emanating from the sources we are observing.

On film, the everyday visual experience is fractured, and the brain must function in a new way to "reconstruct" a continuous visual image. On television, the real-life visual image is fractured in a far more radical way. If we were to set up a series of two thousand still cameras focused on a TV, each shooting at one two-thousandth of a second and firing sequentially (so that we would cover a one-second time span completely), no single camera would record a picture. *The image we "see" on television is never there.* A still camera, shooting at one two-thousandth of a second, will capture only a few dots of light or perhaps a single line across the television. In everyday visual experience, of course, a still photograph of a landscape shot at one two-thousandth of a second will capture a complete visual image of the landscape.

A television set creates a visual image by projecting dots of light, one at a time, onto the front screen. The succession of dots moves across the screen and down alternate "lines." In all, there are 525 such lines on American television sets. During each one-fifteenth of a second, the scanning process will have completed two sweeps, once on each alternate set of lines.

In watching television, our eyes function like our ears. They never see a picture, just as our ears never hear a word. The eye receives a few dots of light during each successive millisecond, and sends these impulses to the brain. The brain

Photograph of a television screen shot at 1/30th of a second.

. . . at 1/60th of a second.

. . . at 1/125th of a second.

. . . at 1/250th of a second.

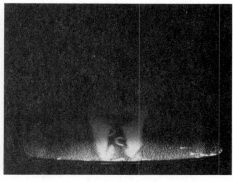

. . . at 1/500th of a second.

records this impulse, recalls previous impulses, and expects future ones. In this way we "see" an image on television. The process differs from film in that it requires much faster processing of information and more visual recall:

1. With film, the brain has to process twenty-four distinct inputs per second. With television, the brain has to process thousands of distinct inputs per second.
2. On a film screen, we always see a complete visual image, even if only for a brief instant (one fiftieth to one seventy-fifth of a second), but the presence of a visual image alternates with periods of nearly equal length in which no image is present. On a television screen, we never see a complete image, since there is never more than a dot of light on the screen at any one time.
3. With film, the brain does not "fill in" the image on the screen—it fills in the motion between the images. With television, the brain must fill in (or recall) 99.999 percent of the image at any given moment, since the full image is never present on the screen.

Watching television, the eye is for the first time functioning like the ear. Film began the process of fracturing visual images into bits of information for the eye to receive and the brain to reassemble, but television completed the transition. For this reason, it is more accurate to say that television is an auditory-based medium. Watching TV, the brain utilizes the eye in the same way it has always used the ear. With television, the patterning of auditory and visual stimuli is identical.

MEDIA AND VIOLENCE

There has been a great concern about the effects of TV on children. If we found more violence only by children against other children, or by children against adults, there might be reason to investigate the harmful influence of TV on children. But the increased violence in our world is among all groups, including adults to other adults, adults to children, and by our society toward other societies. If there is a relation between TV and violence, it must be on a broad societal level, not just in relation to children.

Specific content on TV, in itself, does not foster violence. There has been a good deal of research attempting to show a stimulus-response relation between seeing an act of violence on TV and imitating that behavior in real life. Although some psychologists have managed to create this effect in a controlled laboratory situation, there is no evidence in society's laboratory that supports such a conclusion. There is no increase in the number of gasoline stations robbed the day after thirty-six million people watch such a robbery on "Ironside." And the news coverage of a skyjacking or murder does not *cause* others to imitate this behavior.

TV fosters violence, first, by conditioning people to respond instantly to stimuli in their everyday lives, and by focusing people's attention on the current moment. On TV, the only thing that exists is the current, momentary dot of light or sound vibration—each exists for a millisecond. People develop an orientation to everyday life based on the patterning of electronic information. We become very impatient in situations where information does not move at electronic speed. And we process new information instantly, rather than think out decisions. The increased violence in our society is generated by *impulsive reactions* to stimuli in a situation. This is largely a perceptual problem. We seek meaning in the world that conforms to the perceptual patterning of electronic media.

Second, *constant* exposure to TV over a period of time, and the *sharing* of TV stimuli by everyone in the society, creates a reservoir of common media experiences that are stored in our brains. In a group situation, commonly shared media experiences may overpower the previous nonmedia experiences of each member of the group as the basis on which a collective response will be formulated. The same is true for interpersonal encounters that must later be communicated to many people.

It is easier to explain or justify action based on some experience we share with others. For example, in a political demonstration, there may be a flare-up between a policeman and one demonstrator. Seeing this, other demonstrators may refer the incident to the body of stored personal experiences where similar incidents took place. Their previous personal experiences will all be different, and therefore are not likely to foster an instantaneous collective response. However, if they refer what they see to previous media experiences of seeing demonstrations (commonly shared by all who watch TV), a collective reaction is more likely. Furthermore, since TV tends to show violent moments in demonstrations, the stored media experiences of people in the crowd makes violence commonly available to everyone in the group—as an appropriate collective reaction.

In addition, media depiction of *the good life* as *typical* throughout our society contradicts the everyday experiences of many people. This can be an element conducive to violent behavior, when people who do not experience *the good life* attempt to get *what everyone has*. Here too, constant exposure to TV makes certain solutions to this dilemma *commonly available*. The important point here is that we will get nowhere if we try to establish a direct cause-and-effect relationship between TV and violence in society. TV has a very mild effect in one sense—it makes certain knowledge available to us. The strength of the effect lies in TV's ability to make this knowledge available to everyone.

TRUTH IS A PRINT ETHIC

Truth, as a social value, is a product of print. In preliterate tribal cultures, the truth or falsity of a statement is not as important as whether it conforms to the religious and social beliefs of the society. Similarly, during the greater part of the Middle Ages, an imprimatur by the Church superseded any question of truth or validity regarding printed material. As print became a mass medium, literacy emerged as a social value. In order to learn about the world and communicate this knowledge to others, a person had to be literate. But men soon realized that print information, unlike other sensory data, could be true or false, fiction or nonfiction. Philosophers and *men of letters* spent a great deal of time and energy on this question, and truth emerged as an important social value (though the "white lie" was reserved for those occasions when another social value took precedence over truth). They did not recognize that truth is a particular problem in one medium of communication: the printed word.

No one ever asked of a Steichen photograph, "Is it true or false?" And no one would apply a truth standard in analyzing a Picasso painting. Yet no one would argue that a painting or photograph cannot communicate important and powerful meaning. Likewise, the question of truth is largely irrelevant when dealing with electronic media content. People do not watch "Bonanza" to find out about the Old West. So it makes no sense to ask if the program is a true depiction of that historical period. And we could not ask whether a children's cartoon program is true.

We can and should ask about the effects of television and radio programming. Electronic communication deals primarily with effects. The problem is that no "grammar" for electronic media effects has been devised. Electronic media have been viewed merely as extensions of print, and therefore subject to the same grammar and values as print communication. The patterned auditory and visual information on television or radio is not "content." Content is a print term, subject to the truth-falsity issue. Auditory and visual information on television or radio are stimuli that affect a viewer or listener. As stimuli, electronically mediated communication cannot be analyzed in the same way as print "content." A whole new set of questions must be asked, and a new theory of communication must be formulated.

The problem of applying a truth-falsity paradigm to electronic communication is illustrated most clearly in the case
of advertising. Periodically, the Federal Trade Commission
clamps down on advertisers, demanding that they substantiate
the truthfulness of their claims. How, they ask, can three different headache remedies claim to get into the bloodstream
the fastest? And how can *every* brand of toothpaste claim to
make teeth whiter than *any other* brand of toothpaste? Advertising agencies, forked tongue in cheek, respond by assur-
ing the FTC that truth is essential if they are to convince the
public to buy a product. Ironically, the ad agencies are very
much concerned with truth, but they simply want to *appear*
truthful. However, both the FTC and the agencies are dealing with an irrelevant issue. Neither understands the structure
of electronic communication. They are dealing with TV and
radio as extensions of print media, with the principles of literacy setting the ground rules for truth, honesty, and clarity.

Many advertising agencies believe that if a claim is accepted
as true, the product will be considered better than all others in
the field, thus increasing sales. The continuing proliferation
of words like "best," "most," "cleanest," "purest," "whitest,"
etc., testify to the agency proclivity for leaning on a truth
image. For years, the agencies produced ads that made in-
credible claims for products, and that created arbitrary product differences where none in fact existed. The effect of such
advertising was to produce a general cynicism in the public
mind regarding all radio and television advertising. Perhaps to
combat this, many large agencies recently adopted a policy of
faking "straight talk" in commercials. That is, since the effect
of their commercials was to create a negative attitude toward
the product being advertised, maybe they could use a tone of
voice that would sound truthful. Of course, the result has not
been "straight talk," but announcers who sound like they are
faking "straight talk."

The only important question for the FTC and advertising
agencies alike is: What are the effects of electronic media ad-

It's
New!
the only
brand-new
first
fastest
full-size
great
strong
cleaner
better
The best way
still the best.
BEST THING
brings out the best

vertising? For an advertiser, the issue of concern should center on how the stimuli in a commercial interact with a viewer's real-life experiences and thus affect his behavior in a purchasing situation. Here the key is to connect products to the real lives of human beings. As long as the connection is made in a deep way, and as long as the experience evoked by the commercial is not in conflict with the experience of the product, purchase is possible, or probable. At the moment, agencies could skirt an end run right around the FTC by producing commercials that get to the heart of the human use of products. People take aspirin because they need relief from a headache, not because it has monodyocycolate in it. People enjoy soup for much simpler reasons than the Heinz commercials would lead one to believe. Eating Heinz soup does not give one the feeling that he is part of a 102-piece band riding on top of a gargantuan can of Heinz soup. Commercials that do not connect and resonate with real-life experiences build an incredibility gap for everyone who uses the medium.

From the FTC point of view, "telling the truth" should be the least important social concern. If electronic communication deals with effects, then government agencies responsible for safeguarding public well-being should concern themselves with understanding the effects of a commercial, and preventing those effects that are not in the public interest. A recent television commercial for children's aspirin was 100 percent truthful by the most rigid FTC standard, but the *effect* of the commercial was to make children feel that aspirin is something to take when they want to have a good time. The commercial clearly demonstrates that truth is a print ethic, not a standard for ethical behavior in electronic communication. In addition, the influence of electronic media on print advertising (particularly the substitution of photographic techniques for copy to achieve an effect) raises the question of whether truth is any longer an issue in magazine or newspaper ads.

At present, we have no generally agreed-upon social values and/or rules that can be readily applied in judging whether the effects of electronic communication are beneficial, acceptable, or harmful. Our print-based conception of electronic media prevents us from making social decisions based on a correct understanding of our new communication environment.

TOWARD A RESONANCE THEORY OF COMMUNICATION

In discussing electronically based communication processes, it is very helpful to use auditory terms. Words like *feedback* . . . *reverberation* . . . *tuning* . . . *overload* . . . *regeneration* . . . *fading* describe many of the characteristics of social behavior in relation to electronic media. Similarly, the elements of electronic auditory systems serve as useful analogies for social communication problems. In a public address system, for example, too much output produces feedback. This "fed back" sound becomes reamplified until the system overloads, producing distortion. Someone using such a system must learn to control the output and anticipate feedback. In mass communication, we experience a parallel problem. The interaction of program output with audience feedback can easily produce an information overload.

These analogies suggest a new theory of electronic communication, based on the patterning of information inherent in auditory communication. Transportation theory assumes that communication is difficult to achieve and that a message encounters resistance at each step in its movement across space, over a period of time. In our electronic communication environment, it is no longer meaningful to assume that communication is a low-efficiency process, or that messages must be pushed across a vast chasm in order to be received and understood. The space between phoning from one room in a house to another room in the same house is equivalent to the space between a caller in New York talking to someone in London. In both instances, space has no effect on the flow of information. Similarly, time is no longer relevant when communication takes place at electronic speed, and editing of film, sound, and video tape replaces the linear sequence of events *in time* with events juxtaposed in a time relationship established by the communicator.

In formulating a new theory of communication, it is valuable to build on Ray Birdwhistell's finding that a state of communication is nearly always present in our environment. This state of communication is like an electric circuit that is always turned on. The juice is present in the line, and our problem is to make the current behave in such a way as to achieve the desired effect. Today, there is a nearly constant flow of information at all times. Indeed, one has to expend considerable effort hypothesizing a situation in our culture in which communication does not regularly occur. We take in electronically mediated auditory and visual information as part of our life process. It is part of our immediate physical surround, and we sit in it, absorbing information constantly. The vital question to be posed in formulating a new theory of communication is: What are the characteristics of the process whereby we organize, store, and act upon the patterned information that is constantly flowing into our brain? Further, given these processes, how do we tune communication to achieve the desired effect for someone creating a message?

In electronically mediated human communication, the function of a communicator is to achieve a state of resonance with the person receiving visual and auditory stimuli from television, radio, records, etc. Decoding symbolic forms such as pennants, drums, lantern signals, or written words is no longer our most significant problem. Words transform experience into symbolic forms. They extract meaning from perception in a manner prescribed by the structure of the language, code this meaning symbolically, and store it in the brain. But the brain does not store everything in this way. Many of our experiences with electronic media are coded and stored in the same way that they are perceived. Since they do not undergo a symbolic transformation, the original experience is more directly available to us when it is recalled. Also, since the experience is not stored in a symbolic form, it cannot be retrieved by symbolic cues. It must be evoked by a stimulus that is coded in the same way as the stored information is coded.

The critical task is to design our package of stimuli so that it resonates with information already stored within an individual and thereby induces the desired learning or behavioral effect. Resonance takes place when the stimuli put into our communication evoke *meaning* in a listener or viewer. That which we put into the communication has no meaning in itself. The meaning of our communication is what a listener or viewer *gets out* of his experience with the communicator's stimuli. The listener's or viewer's brain is an indispensable component of the total communication system. His life experiences, as well as his expectations of the stimuli he is receiving, interact with the communicator's output in determining the meaning of the communication.

A listener or viewer brings far more information to the communication event than a communicator can put into his program, commercial, or message. The communicator's problem, then, is not to get stimuli across, or even to package his stimuli so they can be understood and absorbed. Rather, he must deeply understand the kinds of information and experiences stored in his audience, the patterning of this information, and the interactive resonance process whereby stimuli evoke this stored information.

The resonance principle is not totally new or unique to electronic communication. It has always been an element in painting, music, sculpture, and, to a limited degree, even in print. However, resonance is now a more *operational* principle for creating communication because much of the material stored in the brains of an audience is also stored in the brain of a communicator—by virtue of our shared media environment. Also, the *process* of evoking information is quite different today. It is much like the difference between riding a motorcycle under or over ninety miles per hour. Under ninety miles per hour, a driver should turn into a skid. Over ninety miles per hour, he should turn out with the skid. The physical forces working on a skidding motorcycle are reversed as the cycle crosses this speed barrier, so the driver has to reverse his behavior to pull out of the skid. Similarly, in communicating at electronic speed, we no longer direct information into an audience, but try to evoke stored information out of them, in a patterned way.

In the 1930s, a picture of a factory with smoke billowing from several smokestacks meant "prosperity." Today, the same picture means "pollution."

A photograph, film, tape, or book has no meaning outside the possible contexts in which a person might experience it, or outside the body of stored experiences a person will bring to the situation in making sense of what he sees or hears. The stimulus put into the environment will interact with all the elements present in a listening or viewing situation and become communication only through this resonance process.

To achieve a behavioral *effect*, whether persuading someone to buy a product or teaching a person about history, one designs stimuli that will resonate with the elements in a communication environment to produce that effect. The traditional communication process is thus reversed. A "message" is not the starting point for communicating. It is the final product arrived at after considering the effect we hope to achieve and the communication environment where people will experience our stimuli.

In developing a set of useful principles for communicating, it is necessary to abandon most of the traditional rules we were taught. A resonance approach does not begin by asking, "What do I want to say?" We seek to strike a responsive chord in people, not get a message across. This involves, first, examining how stored experiences are patterned in our brain, and how previous experiences condition us to perceive new stimuli. Second, we must understand the characteristics of the new communication environment, and how people use media in their lives. Only at the final stage do we consider the content of a *message,* and this will be determined by the effect we want to achieve and the environment where our content will take on meaning.

PATTERNING OF STORED AUDITORY EXPERIENCES

People are most capable of receiving and understanding sounds they have heard before. A person responds most readily to sounds that evoke past experiences stored in his mind and available for recall. We hear a sound or word and associate it with similar sounds or words already experienced. Moreover, response to stimuli is conditioned by listening habits acquired from past experiences with the stimuli in various contexts. These listening habits interact with stored experiences to create a perceptual resonance that attunes us to receive certain messages in certain ways. We have all had the experience of walking down a street filled with the sounds of cars and trucks and buildings under construction, when one sound broke through. Maybe it was one workman calling another by a nickname (perhaps your nickname), or simply a colloquialism we haven't heard in a while. And perhaps it was said in a particular manner we had heard before, e.g., a rising volume accompanied by an uncharacteristic drop in pitch.

A sound may evoke one set of responses in the first moments of listening, then shift radically as we gather new information from other sensory modes. The new information allows us to refer the entire event to a larger set of stored experiences, where it may take on a different meaning. Thus a woman's voice may evoke an initial unpleasant response, but as we observe her body movement interacting with voice qualities, our reaction may become positive. Similarly, the sound of a fire engine may annoy us at first, then take on a very different meaning as we detect the odor of smoke filtering through our walls.

We know that certain physiological and psychological states may excite specific forms of vocal behavior. A person who has just witnessed a murder talks differently from someone who is relaxing in a living room. Hearing this vocal behavior, we may recognize it as symptomatic of joy, fear, depression, etc., and respond to the perceived condition rather than the words. Thus an announcer who is required by law to state how many calories are in a dessert topping may say the commercial copy with the tone of voice of a sympathetic father giving his daughter permission to eat some candy, thus conveying the meaning associated with the tone of voice rather than the words themselves.

We normally hear sounds at different volumes and develop expectations of a *natural* volume for a given sound in relation to the contexts in which we previously experienced it, and the context in which we are currently hearing it. A person who consistently sits in the front at concerts finds the volume at the back *lower* than a person who consistently sits in the rear. Similarly, different volumes may be perceived as identical when the context is changed. A person in the suburbs may have an ambient sound level in his living room (i.e., sounds that are generally present in the room—an air-conditioner sound, steam moving through the radiator, traffic sounds filtering through the window, etc.) of 40 decibels. If he adjusts the volume on his stereo so that the lowest sound on a record is above the level of ambient sound in the room, the loudest sound on a record may reach 100 decibels. This will create a listening volume in his home that feels like listening in a concert hall. In a city environment, however, the ambient sound level in a living room may be 55 or 60 decibels. Here, if we adjust the volume so that the lowest sound will peak at 110 or 115 decibels, the listener will again experience a volume like the concert hall. The measurable volume levels in the two instances (city vs. suburb) are different, but the listening experiences are equivalent.

The volume of sound in everyday life is affected by the sequence of which it is a part. A sound may be preceded or succeeded by other sounds at low or high volumes. A bottle, shattering as it hits a garbage can, will not ordinarily startle us if a diesel truck has just passed. The same bottle, shattering on a quiet street at night, will affect us quite differently. A telephone ring usually does not startle us, but it can if we are concentrating on a faint scratching sound in a nearby wall where we suspect a mouse is building a home.

Volume is also relative to acoustic setting. A crowded room soaks up sound. Bathroom reverberation provides us with the

Both the volume of speech produced by a speaker and the quality of speech heard by a listener will be different in each of these environments.

experience of hearing our voice as we speak. In addition, volume can be reduced or amplified by competition with other sounds. We have all sat on a quiet beach listening to waves break over a reef, only to be joined by someone with a transistor radio. Conversely, we have heard a clock pop out of the background when we turn off a radio at night.

In each of these cases, a seemingly measurable quality such as volume is dependent on the context in which it occurs. We cannot simply look at the volume being put into the environment, but must study the listening situation in which the stimuli will take on meaning.

If we seek to communicate a situation or event, our problem is not to capture the *reality* of that situation, but to record or create stimuli that will affect the home listener or viewer in a manner similar to a listener's or viewer's experience in the real situation. What counts is not reality, as a scientist might measure it, but the ability to communicate the situation in a believable, human way.

Working in electronic communication, the problems we encounter in communicating "reality" can be rather complex. For example, in creating stimuli for the home environment, one must closely examine differences in *scale* between the situation we are capturing and the typical home where the stimuli will be received. The scale or size of recorded sound is determined by an interaction among many elements: the volume at which sound is performed or spoken in the specific environment where the recording is made; microphone placement in the recording process; the volume at which the recording is played back on the speakers in the specific environment where the listener experiences it; and the distance of a listener from the speaker in the playback environment. If an opera singer, performing at normal volume in a small hall, is recorded in such a way as to capture his or her full volume, and if this recording is played back in our homes with sufficient amplification to re-create the hall performance, there is no problem of scale difference. The *size* of the singer in our home will be equiva-

lent to his or her *size* for a person in the hall. However, if the
same recording is played back at lower volume, the size of the
singer will be too small for the size of the room in which it is
being played.

Most broadcast music is, of course, played in the home at a
much lower volume than was present in the environment
where the sound was created. Size differentials can become
a serious problem. A singer who dazzles the studio audience
on "The Johnny Carson Show" may have a very different effect
on the home audience, listening to him at low volume on
three-inch speakers. Just as an advertisement for an outdoor
billboard has to be redesigned before it is placed in the New
York *Times,* and again before it is placed in *Reader's Digest,*
the size of recorded sound must be redesigned for the more intimate environments in which it will be played. The early success of the bedroom baritones, Rudy Vallee, Russ Colombo,
Bing Crosby, Frank Sinatra, and Perry Como, may be attributed, in part, to the appropriate size of their voice for home
radios and phonographs. They were among the first to sing for
the home environment rather than the old performance hall
environment.

Frequently, the expected interval or space between sounds
affects perception. We expect to hear a space between telephone rings. If I record a telephone ringing and then cut out
the space between rings, so that I have one continuous ring, a
listener would have great difficulty identifying it. Similarly, if
I record speech, and cut out the intervals between words and
sentences, an extraordinary amount of information would be
lost. When our expectation of space between two sounds is not
fulfilled, we have difficulty matching the sound against previous experiences in which the space existed. Thus pause, interval, and silence do not represent the absence of communication. We have patterned expectations for when sound should
not occur, and apply these patterns in making sense of the
space between sounds.

We often use interval to determine the speed of an object.

We compare the intervals between the sound of pistons firing in a car with previous experiences of hearing pistons fire in cars whose speeds we know. In general, a listener expects that less space between sounds indicates faster motion. For example, in the sound of a boxer hitting a punching bag, there is less space between thuds as the bag moves faster and faster. The criteria people use to make these judgments may not be reliable. Simply hearing pistons fire does not tell us if the car is in gear, and the interval between footsteps interacts with a person's stride in determining his walking speed.

The communicator must be aware of the attachments people will make between his stimuli and their previous experiences. The *accuracy* or reality of our stimuli is often less important in determining their ultimate meaning than the pattern listeners will apply in making sense of something they hear. If we know what an audience expects, we can fulfill or disrupt their expectation on purpose, for a purpose. It was a common vaudeville routine to pull the trigger of a gun (with a distinct clicking sound) and have the shot go off several seconds later. Audiences delighted in this gross violation of expected interval. However, the Chinese used the slow dripping of water, whose interval cannot quite be predicted, as a torture. Slow-dripping water defies our attempt to apply a pattern of expectation that will account for the space between drips. Most commonly, the violation of expected interval brings something into prominence. A hammering sound affects us most when it stops or when the person hammering changes pace. A carpenter, working with a new assistant after several months with someone else, will hear the new assistant's hammering—whereas the old assistant seemed to make no sound at all. The pace of the hammering will be different, and it will require some time before he can absorb the pattern of the new hammering sound as part of his environment, rather than attend the sound as new auditory information.

By carefully studying patterns of expectation, we can control or plan how people will react to our stimuli. Bob Marcato, one of the most successful announcers in television commercials, has mastered the possible meanings that can be attached to interval in speech. The secret to his approach rests on understanding *moment to moment* what people expect in each subsequent moment, then pausing for a shorter or longer interval, depending on the effect desired. In Marcato's case, extraordinary training is required to control intervals in *real-time* performance. The same elements can be manipulated through editing of recorded performance, and several variations in interval may be compared to achieve the desired effect.

The distance at which we listen or speak establishes another contextual layer that gives meaning to stimuli. We are put off by someone who speaks directly into our face about a nonpersonal subject, or with a tone of voice we might expect from someone standing ten feet away. Edward T. Hall, an expert on "proxemic" behavior, discusses two key distances: a personal zone (generally, up to five feet) and a social zone (generally, five to twelve feet) (*The Hidden Dimension*, Doubleday Anchor, 1969). In talking, we assign distances to specific subjects and relationships. Sex is discussed predominantly in the personal zone, unless the setting is a classroom lecture—in which case the relationship (teacher-student) would call for a social distance. Normally, we buy meat at a butcher shop from a social distance, unless we would like him to extend credit. Here the relationship might influence us to lean over the counter slightly and thus enter a personal zone. On TV and radio, most performers are speaking in a personal space relationship to home listeners, even though they are separated by thousands of miles. The effective distance between performer and listener is the sum of the distances from the performer's mouth to the microphone, plus the distance from the TV or radio in the home to a listener's ear.

Speaking distance interacts with volume and tone of voice. The skilled actor knows, from accumulated experience, how to change his voice for a radio microphone eight inches away, a television microphone three feet away, and a live audience

forty feet away. The individual who impresses us as having a *commanding personality* is frequently someone who speaks in a social zone but whom we experience as if he were speaking in a personal zone. It may be the case that we can compensate for the loss of visual, olfactory, and tactile information present in communication at a two- or three-foot distance, by translating these sensory data into voice qualities when speaking at a ten- or twenty-foot distance. This ability to translate personality into sound is one of the reasons why one teacher seems to *shout* at students, while another teacher (using similar volume) *speaks* to them.

On radio and television, the translation of multisensory information into sound, or sound and visual images, may be designed and controlled. This is not to say that a particular camera angle can represent a smell, or that holding a microphone very close to the source of sound will create tactile sensation. In electronic communication, one uses the body of stored tactile and olfactory experiences in a listener or viewer to *fill in* such sensations when seeing or hearing our stimuli. We cannot create a sound that smells like food, but we can organize sounds that will evoke past experiences where similar experience of sounds accompanied the smell of food. If we can deeply associate our stimuli with those experiences, a listener will recall the smell as well as the sound and thus experience the commercial stimuli as if they contained olfactory information.

The terms "hot" and "cool" have been used widely to indicate generic media characteristics and/or the personality qualities of someone who appears on a given medium. However, one cannot determine the *temperature* of a medium, or someone's performance on it, without understanding the total communication context. In determining whether Johnny Carson's per-

formance is cool, it will make a great deal of difference if you are sitting eighteen inches, six feet, or twenty feet from the screen; what size screen you are watching; what size Carson is on the screen; and the distance from Carson's mouth to his microphone. For example, Carson's success as a host is based, in part, on the fact that he is always closer to a microphone than any of his guests. He is thus *closer* to the home listener and can more easily regulate interaction between guests and the home audience.

Similarly, one cannot compare the relative temperatures of TV and film and radio without comparing the typical listener-viewer distance for TV and film and radio, as well as how many are watching each medium and under what conditions.

If one applies the general understanding of "hot" and "cool" to a performer like Fidel Castro, he seems all wrong for television. His speeches are too long. He shouts frequently, and his

Carson's voice is picked up by a microphone directly in front of him . . .

. . . A guest's voice is picked up by an overhead microphone not visible on-camera.

In many parts of the world TV is viewed in public places. Here, villagers in Ninhquoi, South Vietnam, watch an outdoor community television set. (Photo by Claude Johner, the New York *Times*.)

visual image is too hot for a cool medium like television. Then why does he remain in power, if he does not use television correctly? For one thing, his television performance is taking place in a different culture, and a listener-viewer's judgment of hot or cool will vary among cultures. Equally important, Cuban television is commonly viewed in parks or public places where the audience distance is considerably greater than the typical audience distance for U.S. television. Unlike an American politician on television, where the typical listener-viewer is three to ten feet from his set, Castro's TV performance is rather analogous to a politician speaking in a hall to an audience fifteen to thirty feet away. The variations in listener distance between Cuban and American audiences require totally different behavior by the performer.

The listening or viewing situation where stimuli take on meaning, and the patterning of stored experiences a person brings to a new event in making sense of what he sees or hears, cannot be reduced to a set of hard rules for the communicator to apply. I have discussed a few variables in order to illustrate how one should *approach* the problem, but a list of possible elements that may affect a situation would be endless. One must develop a task orientation that looks at each problem separately, and study those elements that will likely affect our stimuli in each particular situation.

The opening of the Erie Canal . . . occurred on October 26, 1825. On that day, waiting crowds at the Battery heard, rolling down the broad Hudson, the roar of a cannon. One minute later, a thirty-two-pounder was fired at the Battery, followed at one-minute intervals by discharges at Governor's Island, Forts Lafayette and Richmond, and Sandy Hook. . . . As Morse was still painting portraits, and Bell and Marconi were not yet born, the managers of the celebration were justly proud of the fact that Buffalo had communicated with Sandy Hook in the amazingly short time of one hundred minutes.

Rodman Gilder
The Battery
Houghton Mifflin, 1936

In the past, most of the sounds that affected our lives—the sound of children playing on the street, a mother calling out a window, or a storekeeper talking—reached our ears through the medium of air, traveling at 1,130 feet per second. Today, sound is transmitted primarily by radio waves and electricity, at 186,000 miles per second, nearly one million times faster.

In the past, even under the most elaborate conditions, a "shot heard 'round the world" took days. News of Lincoln's assassination required weeks or months for transmission around the world. Reactions to this news required equal time. Yet the sound of the gunshot killing Lee Harvey Oswald could travel everywhere in a fraction of a second. Indeed, it is estimated that President Kennedy's assassination was known by more than 70 percent of the American population within a half hour. Today, it is common for major news events to be transmitted throughout the world in a few minutes. As a result, political and military interactions take place very quickly. Most important, this characteristic of the new environment eliminates the *time between* receiving information and responding to it. People do not think out decisions. They respond instantly to stimuli. In the Cuban missile crisis, vital messages between the United States and the Soviet Union were actually ignored by the two governments, and diplomatic maneuvers were undertaken to inhibit the flow of information, because the flow threatened to spiral into a dangerous overload. The flow of information had accelerated beyond the abilities of men governing nations to make responses *demanded* of them because they had such information.

The speed of commonplace sounds has also changed:

MOTHER: Susie . . . Susie . . . come in for lunch. . . .
DAUGHTER: O.K., Mommy. . . .
                    1949 recording of a mother calling out a second-
                    floor window to her daughter on the sidewalk

MOTHER: Amy . . . Amy, dear. . . .
DAUGHTER: Yes, Mommy. . . .
MOTHER: Amy, I'm sending your sweater down with the elevator man. He'll give it to the doorman. You get it from the doorman and put it on now. When your lunch is ready, I'll call you on your radio.
                    1971 recording of a mother on the twentieth
                    floor of a high-rise, calling to her daughter on
                    the sidewalk, via a two-way radio

In the old environment, the volume of sound reaching our ears was directly related to the power of a sound at its source and its distance from us. A sound originating outdoors competed with other outdoor sounds to *get through* to us. Today, sounds reaching us through electricity are less subject to interference from sounds in the outdoor environment, and the volume of sound reaching our ears is controlled by us— we simply turn the volume control on the radio or TV to a desired level.

A mother in 1949 could shout only so far. Her messages were short, and a communication *exchange* with her daughter was difficult. A mother on the twentieth floor today cannot shout out the window and expect to be heard on the sidewalk below. But with a two-way radio, she can talk to her daughter, and a communication exchange is possible. Electricity permits sound to travel much farther without loss of signal strength. As a result, we transmit more information in less time, and reach larger audiences.

Sunday papers . . . *Times, Tribune, American, News, Mirror* . . . get your Sunday papers. . . .

1949 recording of a newsboy
on a street corner

ALAN KING: I start every morning with the New York *Times.* The first thing I do when I get up is read the obituary column. If my name isn't in it, I get dressed.

ANNOUNCER: Comedian Alan King for the New York *Times.* For free home delivery, call MU 7-0700.

1971 recording of a radio
commercial

In the past a newsboy's call was in earshot of relatively few persons, but millions of people shared Alan King's endorsement of the New York *Times.* Electronically mediated communication allows us to share more information with more people. A sizable proportion of our experiences are common to everyone. The common information environment created by television and radio experience standardizes backgrounds and attitudes in everyday life.

I designed a trademark for a letterhead and a few weeks after it was printed, I was looking in a magazine on British design and I saw that another designer had designed exactly the same mark, the same device. That's the thing that scared me. We had somehow gotten the same input and designed this the same way. I realized how overreaching everything has become. I felt that I wasn't really expressing myself, just expressing the stream of everybody's consciousness.

Excerpted from an interview
with Seymour Chwast
Push Pin Studios

Experiences with television and radio stimuli are often more real than first-hand, face-to-face experiences. My wife loves to tell of a neighbor who was sitting in a park with her baby when another woman passed and commented, "Oh, what a beautiful baby." "Yes," replied the neighbor, "but you should see his pictures."

In New Guinea when a village leader is ignored by his people, the Papuan Government sometimes records his speech on tape, then releases it on radio, to be heard by now respectful villagers, played to them by the village leader himself, probably on his own radio.

In the Highlands of New Guinea I saw men with photographs of themselves mounted on their foreheads, in front of their head-feathers. Friends greeted them by examining the photographs.

> Ted Carpenter
> *They Became What They Beheld*
> Outerbridge & Dienstfrey
> New York, 1970

The "captured reality" of television is often preferred to personal experience. Three British reporters, writing about the assassination of Robert Kennedy, noted that as the casket was passing through the airport in New York after arriving from Los Angeles, most of the newsmen present watched the TV monitors of the networks broadcasting the event despite the fact that they were only ten feet from the casket itself.

Joseph Napolitan, a public affairs consultant, tells of a London conference where each speaker was televised on a large screen in the ballroom—so those who did not have a good view of the dais could still see the speaker. He noticed, however, that everyone watched the TV screen, including those directly in front of the dais, who had to turn their heads in order to see the screen.

One of the most extraordinary characteristics of our new electronic environment is that it has created a new form of space: auditory acoustic space. In the old environment, we were very conscious of a sound's *direction*. Having two ears, we can distinguish slight differences in the volume of sound striking the left or right ear, and thereby judge the direction

of a sound. Also, most sounds have a characteristic volume at
the point of output, so the volume reaching our ears often tells
us how far we are from its source. Further, high frequencies
are very directional (they emanate straight out from the
source) and they carry far, while low frequencies are less directional and require more power to reach the same distance.
Having experienced the frequency characteristics of a sound,
we can judge the distance and direction by the frequency

characteristics and volume of the sound as it reaches our ears. Sound in this environment was also *contained* within architectural space. The physical characteristics of a listening environment, whether a living room, concert hall, valley, or forest, affected sounds in that environment. For example, the design of a room and the texture of the six surfaces can impose unwanted reverberation on our listening, and the walls of a valley may create an echo. All of these characteristics attached us to Euclidian space, which has *direction* and *distance.*

In our new environment, more and more of the sounds we hear are electronically mediated and amplified. This has radically affected the structure of sound for listeners and created a new relation between sound and space. Sound need no longer be contained within a physical environment that defines boundaries for the sound. Amplification of sound, particularly in rock music, is so overwhelming that it creates its own walls—walls of sound—that *contain* a listener.

I can't talk about my singing, I'm inside of it.
How can you describe something you're inside of?
                    Janis Joplin
                    quoted from New York *Times Magazine*
                    February 23, 1969

Under these conditions, sound becomes a total surround for the listener, or a space bubble in which the listener bathes in sound. One teen-age girl described her experience this way:

It was just this bubble we were riding along in, just the music and me . . . we were right inside everything and I could just get completely involved in the music.

Under high amplification, the pattern of emanation for low and high frequencies is overwhelmed by the sheer power of

the output. So the frequency characteristics offer no information to a listener regarding direction. Also, since volume is
manipulated electronically, we cannot compare the volume of
sound reaching our ears with the *natural* volume we may
have experienced at the source of the sound during a previous
listening experience, to determine the distance. Further, high
amplification overloads our auditory channel of perception,
blocking out the sensory information that might attach us to
architectural space. Our link with the Euclidian world is thus
dissolved, and we enter auditory acoustic space.

> It's nice to stay indoors and let the music take your head wher-
> ever it wants to go.
>
>   Alison Steele
>   WNEW-FM, New York

Auditory acoustic space has no front or back, no above or
below, no past or future. And it has no linear directionality.
For a listener, sound does not come toward him but is present
everywhere in the space he experiences, and it totally saturates
his sensory receptors. Auditory acoustic space only exists for
the current fleeting moment, and the current fleeting moment
is the only thing that exists for those who enter it. Their relation to time and space is patterned according to their mode of
receiving auditory stimuli.

Auditory acoustic space is more like something we wear or
sit in than a physical area in which we move. A listener is
wrapped in auditory space and reverberates with the sound.
There is clear evidence that the human body actually resonates
with low-frequency sound at high amplification. Often, the
experience is described in terms of tactile sensation, as when
people say they do not so much hear as feel the music. When
the Rolling Stones performed at Madison Square Garden, the
decibel level in the front of the audience reached 136 decibels.
The performance was amplified through 150 speakers deliver-
ing 16,000 watts of power.

High amplification is not the only way to enter auditory acoustic space. The telephone eliminates architectural space between a listener and speaker. Thus a telephone voice never takes on the characteristics of sound moving through air in a room. This is why we experience great difficulty in trying to

visualize the person we are speaking to at the other end of a telephone line. Headphones also eliminate the need for high amplification, since they cut off architectural acoustic information in the listener's environment. Listening on headphones, a person is alone with the music in a space carved by the sound on a record, radio, or tape. This can change his spatial environment instantly and take the listener on a trip. It may be an outer trip, as when the headphones transport him to a concert hall, or it may be an inner trip, as when the sound takes a listener inside himself and gives him the feeling that he is part of the music. Similarly, a transistor radio held close to the ear creates a portable auditory environment, or more accurately, it allows a person to sit in auditory space anywhere he goes.

The auditory space created by this use of radio, TV, or telephone can be carried with us when we travel. Telephones are available just about anywhere. Radio is totally portable, and television is available in bars, motels, waiting rooms, even

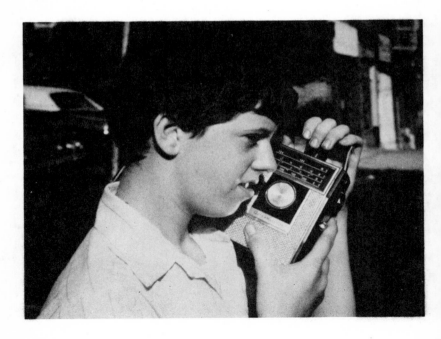

a few cars. Electronic media enable us to carve the same space we live in at home, in cars, office buildings, schools, a friend's house, etc.

> When you take your radio out with you, you're taking part of your home with you . . . you're carrying it. . . . In the car, it's also bringing part of your house with you. And the radio's good there because you can look out and see the scenery, but you don't have to hear the other cars' motors, which isn't too pleasant a sound.
>
> Twelve-year-old

A person visiting or moving to another part of the country can structure the environment in his new home to duplicate his old environment. His spatial relation to sources of information will be quite similar, no matter where he moves. The *change* in one's environment created by moving from a second-floor apartment in a city of eighty thousand to a tenth-floor apartment in a city of eight hundred thousand is minimized by the availability in both situations of the *same* telephone service, radio and TV programming, and stereo listening.

> In the wintertime, we go south for a month or two, and there I can see the same television programs that I have been watching at home in New York City. It makes me feel at home.
>
> Retired woman

The geographic location of an audience has become less meaningful for those who create communication.

In the average American home, TV, radio, or stereo play during virtually all waking hours. Prior to electricity, auditory information in the home was limited to talk and a few sounds that filtered through the windows. The life styles of people oriented to the new environment reflect a broader world. This is demonstrated in the case of the Mott family, a wealthy, socially conscious, family in the Midwest. The elderly father devotes his philanthropic efforts to the city of Flint, Mich. His "world" is the local town where he grew up and continues to live. The son, however, promotes national and international causes: birth control, peace, environmental protection, etc. For the father, face-to-face contact is essential for involvement:

HOW WE SPEND OUR TIME EACH WEEK
(from CBS Research)

Sleeping	53.2	hours
Working	40.0	hours
Watching TV	26.4	hours
Listening to radio	21.2	hours
Eating	8.4	hours
Reading newspapers	4.2	hours
Reading magazines	3.3	hours
Listening to records	1.3	hours
Attending a movie	.2	hour
Reading books	.06	hour
Attending a sporting event	.06	hour
Attending a cultural event	.05	hour

"My father tackles significant problems with a lot of feedback. He's 'Mr. Flint.' He likes that." For the son, a carefully designed advertisement on birth control or arms control substitutes for personal contact. Electricity enabled him to grow up in a larger world, where he receives indirect social feedback (e.g., affecting an opinion poll).

Participation in a broader world through electronic media does not mean less personal involvement. Media serve many personal functions in people's lives. We use media to relax us, pacify us, wake us up, and assure us that the world is still there. Media are used to accompany exercise, bathroom activity, and food preparation. Or media may simply keep us company (Mendelsohn's classic study *Listening to Radio,* treats this function in depth) (in *People, Society, and Mass*

Communications, Dexter and White, eds. The Free Press).

Once media establish a personal involvement between the home audience and Johnny Carson or Walter Cronkite, they maintain the relationship by presenting him in our home every night or at regular intervals each week. People then develop expectations, much like face-to-face friendships, that a television personality or event will come into their homes to cheer them up, tell the latest gossip, or lull them to sleep.

When Denmark began twenty-four-hour-a-day radio programming, the suicide rate dropped:

In a modern society many people wait up at night, and radio has become a sort of companion to them. Many people have stopped worrying about the night, worrying that might lead them to think of suicide or even commit suicide.

> Director of Denmark Radio
> Personal interview

People are more likely to choose programming on the basis of some personal function it serves, rather than for specific content. In many instances, it does not matter what a program is *about.* Totally different content may serve the same function. And two situation comedies about a small-town sheriff in the South may have nothing in common from a functional standpoint. It is curious to observe networks imitating each other's content (e.g., a successful program about a doctor will generate several other doctor programs) when people are watching for reasons that have little to do with the overt subject matter. It is more meaningful to investigate how people *feel* about a TV personality or character in a program than to note that a given number of viewers are watching police dramas, quiz shows, or news programming.

CREATING STIMULI

If you were faced with the problem of selling toothpaste, it would not make much sense to design a commercial for late-night TV that stated, "Now run right down to your corner drugstore and get a tube of Crest."

If you were faced with the problem of convincing inner-city black women to get a Pap test, it would not make much sense to show an upper-middle-class white woman in a suburban doctor's office, where she easily and quickly receives a Pap test. The inner-city black woman's previous experiences in

---

RCA AD RUFFLES POWER STRUCTURE

Earlier this month RCA Records and Tapes ran a full-page ad in The Village Voice and the underground press that did not escape the notice of the above-ground power structure.

Promoting a new album by Lou Reed, "supermusician and legendary city poet," it shows a fellow spray painting Lou's name on the already graffiti-covered wall of a subway car. "Lou Reed makes his mark," is the headline and could have added, "with the New York City Transit Authority and the Parks, Recreation and Cultural Affairs Administration."

Both, in effect, have cried out: cease and desist, the kids don't need that kind of inspiration.

August Heckscher, administrator of Parks, wrote to the president of RCA Records to note his dismay that a company "with its long tradition of public service could be a party to an act of vandalism."

John G. deRoss, general counsel of the T.A. took his case to the top, to Robert W. Sarnoff, RCA chairman. Douglas Alligood, the company's general counsel, responded that RCA shares the T.A.'s concern and he promised that the ad would not run again. Grey Advertising is the agency.

"We used to be autonomous," said a spokesman for RCA Records.

New York *Times*,
May 30, 1972

---

public clinics would render your message unbelievable and *unbearable.*

In each of these cases, our message might be a highly creative rendering of *what we want to say.* However, it would fail to communicate the effect desired. *Before* we create a message, we must focus on the effect desired; the characteristics of the medium to be used; the personal relation between the audience and the media through which they will receive our stimuli, in the situation and at the time they are likely to view or hear it; and the previous experiences of individual members of the audience that can be evoked to generate the effect we desire. Thus when I was asked by the American Cancer Society back in the sixties to create a TV spot that would encourage people to give up smoking, I did not ask, "What can I say to convince people to stop smoking?" Rather, I attempted to evoke feelings based on a listener-viewer's experience that might lead to the desired change in behavior, given the likely context in which my stimuli would be seen and heard. The spot I designed shows two children dressing up in their parents' clothes. At the end, a voice-over announcer says very calmly, "Children love to imitate their parents . . . Children learn by imitating their parents. Do you smoke cigarettes?" The American Cancer Society said it was the most successful spot they ever ran, and they subsequently used the theme in other ads. The antismoking *message* was not in the words or visual of the commercial, but in the *feelings* evoked by the commercial stimuli.

Hard Sell, Soft Sell, Deep Sell

━━━〜〜〜〜〜〜〜〜〜〜━━━

Since TV and radio commercials and print ads have no meaning in themselves, it makes little sense to research them. Advertising functions within an environmental surrounding that gives commercials or ads meaning and determines their effect on consumer purchase of products. It is this environmental surrounding that merits careful research and scrutiny by those who seek to influence consumer behavior.

The environmental surrounding in which we live is structured by electronic media. Radio and television are around all of us all the time, and the same media that surround us, surround everyone in our society. This orientation to electronic sources of information has produced changes in the design of stores, altered purchasing behavior, and transformed the learning process as it relates to advertising.

THE NEW STORE

In the past, it was common for stores to extend into the street or have elaborate window displays. The fruit market

physically extended onto the sidewalk; the barber pole or clothing rack in front of the store signaled the service offered; and the display window told the passer-by what items were inside. Also, there were many pitchmen on the sidewalk who showed us the products they were selling from a cart, or attempted to *pull* us into the store they represented. Today, television and radio perform these same functions in our home.

Now here is a pen that hasn't got the feature of a number on it, but it gives you any sort of line without changing the point. Now if you understand, realize and appreciate a real good value, and if my physiognomy is not too conspicuous to be comprehended, I'm gonna clarify to such an extent that each and every individual standing here at the present time can very well afford it, I'm

gonna give you this Parker 61 type. Now don't forget, you can take my pen into any pawn shop. Ask him for ten dollars, see how quick he chase you out, but you ask him for five dollars he may give it to you. And today I'm not going to charge you no dollar bills for the pen, but the first lady or gentleman who gives me twenty-five cents gets the pen. And I think it's worth a quarter to anyone.

1949 recording of a street corner pen pitchman

No matter how you punish it, a Bic ballpoint writes first time, every time. Bic medium point nineteen cents. Bic fine point twenty-five cents. Bic writes first time, every time.

1971 television commercial

Today most stores no longer extend toward the street. They look inward. Store extensions and sidewalk props have all but disappeared. Many new stores have no display windows. And many older stores leave the same display for years, or let the

window remain empty. Of course, stores whose products are not advertised on radio or TV (e.g., a pawn shop or leather crafts store) retain the old structure. But for many stores, the only external cue that remains important is the sign above the door. And here, many chain stores need only display their name, not the type of goods sold: e.g., *Whalen's* rather than *Whalen's Drugs;* or *McDonald's* rather than *McDonald's Hamburgers.* Manufacturers have recognized this change in store structure:

> There's been a definite decline in the materials produced by manufacturers for windows today. All the material produced for display is produced for inside the store or for shelves or for island displays.
>
> Marketing executive,
Bristol-Myers

Shelf and island displays aid in recalling television and radio commercials. Now that advertising tells people what products are available, the function of a display in the store is to recall the consumer's experience of the product in the commercial. A druggist I interviewed explained:

> Years ago, people would come in and say, "Recommend me something." Today, they know what they want. Television educates them as to what they want to purchase. Different commercials that you hear . . . you hear of a cough medicine on television, they come in after that and they buy the cough medicine.
>
> People want to see and feel what they buy. Years ago they would ask for something. Today, if you don't show them, the product doesn't sell. It's the point of contact that impresses them. You walk into the store and it strikes you right away, and you buy it. If it isn't there, you just forget. That's the difference between a modern and an old store.
>
> Local drugstore owner

If a product is always displayed in a package on a store shelf . . .

. . . the advertiser must be careful not to show it on television exclusively in its unpackaged form.

People do not walk into a store today with a precise, memorized list of items they want to buy. If memory were the basis for buying products, retailing operations would be structured quite differently. Supermarkets, instead of emphasizing aisle space where a consumer walks around and selects what he wants from what he sees, could move a customer to the checkout area immediately upon entering the store. The customer would simply punch out the items desired on a computerized card, and a mechanized stockroom would deliver all the merchandise, wrapped and tabulated for payment. But something else is functioning in the buying situation.

Commercials have created a consumer orientation that re-

New products that are heavily advertised on television no longer re-
quire a name *like Savarin or Maxwell House. Instead, the product*
name *can be a descriptive quality.*

quires the retailer to bring a large percentage of goods out
from the stockroom and into the store. This is the *effect* of
radio and TV commercials: to make the store a stockroom and
the salesperson a checkout clerk. The reason for this may be
traced to the *recall* patterns generated by commercials, in spite
of the advertisers' attempts to work on the conscious *memory*
of the consumer. You don't ask for a product: The product
asks for you! That is, a person's *recall* of a commercial is
evoked by the product itself, visible on a shelf or island display, interacting with stored data in his brain. This process is
quite different from memory, and has crucial implications for
creating commercial stimuli.

How does memory differ from recall? Well, if you ask people to listen to a story, then repeat what they *remember* for someone else, the result may resemble the following grapevine experiment. In this experiment, each person received instructions that he would be told a story, and then asked to repeat it for someone who had not heard it.

The story as told by the experimenter to the first subject:

There was an old man who bought a dog. He took him out to a friend's house by a lake to see if the dog knew any tricks. At the lake he picked up a stick and threw it onto the water. The dog ran across the field and out on the lake, but instead of swimming he walked across the water, picked up the stick, and brought it back to the old man. The old man turned to his friend and said, "Now what do you think of that?" The friend said, "How much did you pay for that dog?" "Five dollars," replied the old man. "Well," said the friend, "you got a real gypping. You bought a dog that can't even swim."

The story as repeated by subject No. 4, after it had been retold by three previous subjects:

What I heard about the dog was that he couldn't swim. But I think he did a good thing, whatever he did. And I love animals above grown old people. Grown people like me and other neighbors of mine always exaggerate, and I detest people when they are liars to themselves. I, once in my life was told by my mother and father, never say anything wrong about other children. If you can't play with them just leave them alone.

The memory process introduces new *errors* at each stage of repeating the story, which cumulatively leads to total distortion. This form of learning (i.e., hearing a story, memorizing it, and repeating it for someone) is not very accurate or efficient. It is subject to the interpretation of each listener, and there-

fore the introduction of *noise* into the original message content (e.g., the fourth subject in the experiment used the opportunity of telling the story, to relate something that was on
her mind at that moment). Too, the ability to understand and
repeat a message varies greatly within a population.

Memory is not the only mental process available for learning. If I were to tell several people, in a variety of listening
contexts, "Because you met me, you'll be different for the rest
of your _____," and ask them to fill in the last word, the simi-
larity of their responses would be very high. In this instance, I
would be structuring the communication environment to evoke
a *recall* mechanism in the listener. My stimulus does not introduce new information. Rather, it resonates with information already within the listener and available for recall. Thus
there is less chance for a listener to interpret it incorrectly or
respond with the wrong word. Furthermore, this type of recall is the fastest function of the brain, while conscious memory
is the slowest.

Most advertisers are unaware of the relation between recall
and our electronic information environment, and therefore depend almost entirely on memory to communicate information
about a product.

ADVERTISING RESEARCH

Most advertising research follows logically, and incorrectly,
from the advertisers' obsolete approach to learning. Advertising
agencies have a central interest in whether people remember
commercials they hear on radio or see and hear on television,
and they are constantly evaluating their commercials by testing people's memory of them. A common testing situation involves a group of women who are paid to watch commercials
projected in a theater environment. After viewing the commercials, they fill out questionnaires that measure their recollection of details or absorption of product image. The truth-

fulness and honesty of the responses cannot be verified, nor can they accurately measure the degree to which a respondent is capable or incapable of self-reporting his or her reactions. Furthermore, the researchers narrowly focus their questions on a subject's recollection of commercial *content*, which they consider the essence of what makes a message effective. *Content* is synonymous with scripted visuals, actor dialogue, and announcer copy (in essence, what the creator tried to *put into* the commercial). No effort is made to test the effects of camerawork, sound design, information stored in a viewer that might resonate with the commercial stimuli, or the critical elements in a listening or viewing situation that will give the commercial meaning (in essence, what a person *gets out* of the commercial). For example, when the station is about to break for a commercial, the announcer will say, "A report about the war coming right up." We then see two or three commercials before hearing about the war. This is a self-defeating practice, first because it makes the commercial an *interruption* of news, and second, because the commercial prevents those who might have a personal interest in the war from hearing it immediately.

Advertising researchers are not able to control situation variables, whether it is the programming before or after a commercial, the time of day when a spot is run, or the elements in a listener's home that will affect what he gets out of the commercial stimuli. One agency, worried about the artificial qualities of theater testing in relation to home viewing, attempted to simulate a *natural* listening environment by asking women to view commercials in a trailer parked near a shopping center.

This type of testing is of little value, primarily because it is directed toward measuring what a viewer remembers in relation to a commercial, not how people are affected by a commercial message in their home environment where they actually view it or the store environment where the actual purchase will take place. Advertisers are testing in the same way my daughter is tested in the fourth grade. Both the commercial viewer and the fourth-grader are shown visual information or are asked to listen to some comments, and are subsequently quizzed in a formal manner about what they remember. The form of learning being measured has no direct relation to behavior. Social behavior, whether it takes the form of buying a product, developing friendships, or rioting, is determined by a much greater store of experiences in our brain than is available to conscious remembering. Certain stimuli, in the proper context, can recall experiences that we could never remember at will.

Ad agencies generally use a transportation theory of communications. They are trying to get information across to people, to sink it into their brains. And they use research to measure what they have implanted in a person's mind. What ad agencies seek to measure after they have produced a commercial, I need to know, in my commercial work, before I start. I do not care what number of people *remember* or *get* the message. I am concerned with how people are affected by the stimuli.

INFORMATION AVAILABLE FOR RECALL

The total amount of information imprinted or coded within our brains is huge, and the associations that can be generated by evoked recall are very deep. Information available for recall includes everything we have experienced, whether we consciously remember it or not. This total body of stored material is always with us, and it surrounds and absorbs each new learning experience. Furthermore, it is instantly recallable when cued by the appropriate stimulus.

The evoked recall process is similar to the experience of seeing an automobile accident. In witnessing an accident, you hear the squeal of brakes, the crash of the car, and possibly see a person bleeding. At a later time, should you hear the squeal of brakes you may also recall many of the sights, sounds, feelings, and associations you experienced earlier. You will recall the event instantly, and this recall will form part of the context that gives meaning to the present stimulus. In the same way, if the advertiser evokes human feelings and human experiences in relation to a product in a commercial, the next time we see the product in a store, there is a good chance it will evoke the associations experienced with the commercial.

An important qualification should be entered here. In a commercial context, one cannot develop unbelievable associations between a product and real-life situations and expect to evoke past experiences in a viewer or listener that will support the attachment of the product to those experiences. That is, a viewer has no past experience of feeling like a king because he likes the taste of margarine, or having women attempt to seduce him when he changed hair tonics. An advertiser's research should deeply explore the *actual* experiences people

have with products in real-life situations, and structure stimuli in the commercials in such a way that the real-life experience will be evoked by the product when the consumer encounters it in a store.

If you are selling a kitchen drain cleaner, the advertising effort might involve building an association in the listener's mind between the *real* annoyance of a stopped-up sink and the *real* relief of unclogging it, in the context of using the product. If the commercial is effective, seeing the product in a store will evoke the consumer's feelings about clogged sinks and thereby generate a purchase of the product, to correct his or her stopped-up sink problem at home. The association could be made by having a woman, not necessarily a real housewife, reacting to a stopped-up sink in a *believable* way (believability is more important than reality). I am not talking about a "Josephine the plumber" type. If the advertiser can render a deep commercial on the feelings of a believable woman after she unstopped a sink that had been troubling her for several days, a real experience is created for the listener or viewer, and it will be stored permanently in his or her brain. When the consumer sees the product in the store, whether he or she consciously remembers it or not, the product may evoke the experience of the commercial. If that experience was meaningful, and there is a need, the consumer is likely to buy the product. Furthermore, if the consumer's expectation is then fulfilled by experience with the product, you have a customer who will come back again.

Advertising typically attempts to influence the consumer by *teaching* him the name of a product and hoping he will remember it when he goes to the store. But if we make a deep attachment to the product in the commercial, there is no need to depend on their remembering the name of the product. Seeing the product in the store should evoke the association attached to the product in the commercial. As the drugstore owner quoted previously said, "It strikes you."

Sometimes commercials inadvertently use a primitive version

of the process I am describing. These commercials do not utilize the real-life associations people have with the product. Rather, they create slogans or "unique selling propositions" to achieve a *name identification* effect. Given no other reason to buy product X as opposed to product Y, this vague feeling of familiarity with the name or slogan may be sufficient to induce purchasing product X. Endless repetition of a commercial may produce a similar effect. That is, while the ad content attempts to make the product unique, the running of the ad makes the product commonplace and environmental.

If one approaches a commercial from the base I am outlining, the role of *testing* becomes one of measuring people's behavior in the store. It is irrelevant to study whether people remember a product after seeing a commercial. The researcher could better concern himself with consumer action and reaction when he or she sees the product on display.

The function of advertising is to give the consumer materials and associations that he can recall in purchasing situations. A commercial should attach those meaningful associations that will be evoked by the stimulus of seeing the product in a store. Store design, package design, and marketing strategies should provide a context that is most likely to induce evoked recall. Effective advertising must encompass this total process.

DESIGNING A COMMERCIAL

Those of us who create commercials are in the business of structuring recall. When audience recall is effectively structured, the audience becomes an active part of the communication process.

One of the major changes that has come into the world with the electronic environment as a total surround is that the audience becomes a work force instead of being target for campaigns.
                                                    Marshall McLuhan
                                                    Personal recording

When the audience is viewed as a work force in the communication process, the experiences and attitudes people bring to
a viewing or listening situation become active elements in our
advertising effort. Under these conditions, we know that the
content of media includes far more than the visual and auditory information in the commercial itself. The wealth of
stored information contained within the brains of members of
the audience interacts with the stimuli presented by the advertiser in creating the total content of the commercial. It is
for this reason the old Salem commercial could leave out the
final phrase in their jingle, "You can take Salem out of the
country, but . . .", once it had saturated our information environment. The audience served as a work force for the commercial and filled in the final phrase.

As the media speed up the information flow in our society
and allow everyone to share the same information, the ability
to *participate by feedback* on the part of an audience is increased. In an amazingly short time, the average viewer will
recognize a new commercial campaign, identify the variations
among different commercials within the campaign, and develop
responses (often, puns or caricatures of an actor's voice) to
specific lines or situations in the spot. Indeed, most commercials *burn into* the public's mind long before they are taken
off the air:

I'm in my store and I see customers all day long. After Walter
Cronkite's had the news on the night before and has given us
a sensational story, the customers will tell me about it. They do
have the details, they have them correctly.

Still, the same news agents who put on the Walter Cronkite
news show turn around and give these same people who can get
the story *once* very effectively, these same news people will give
us a commercial over and over again, forty times the same commercial. I don't understand how they think we have one kind of
mind for the news and another kind for commercials.

Liquor store owner

For a commercial designer, this speedup in rate of absorption (and indignation when they notice a commercial being repeated over and over) has many practical implications. After running a sixty-second commercial a few times, we can easily substitute a designed-down thirty-second version of the spot with minimal loss in effect. Also, we can take a campaign that has been running for some time and design a new campaign with pieces from the old. This can evoke the audience's experience with the old campaign as well as build new associations with the product. For example, I have redesigned old Coke spots into a totally new campaign. In some of these spots, the word "Coke" was not even mentioned, yet the attachment of the commercial associations to the product was quite deep.

More fundamentally, the liquor store owner's comment suggests that a properly designed commercial need only be run a sufficient number of times to reach the intended audience *once*. It may be run over a long period, since new groups of people will encounter the problem or develop a need for the product as time goes on, but within any fixed period of time they need to see an effective commercial only once.

Suppose, for example, that you are about to buy a car and are having trouble making a decision. If, during this period, you see a commercial that touches deeply on the problem you are experiencing, you will be inclined to resonate with it. By tuning into your problem, the commercial will induce deep participation and generate positive feedback. Viewing the commercial once can accomplish this, and multiple viewings will not significantly strengthen the effect.

THE MEDIA ENVIRONMENT FOR COMMERCIALS

Because electronic media are part of our environment, we do not consciously perceive them as a *mediating* factor in the flow of information. We are so involved with electronic media that we are not aware of their effect upon us. If you ask people how specific media function in their daily lives, you find they are most accurate in reporting on those media with which they are *least* involved. For example, they will tend to report most accurately concerning newspapers and magazines. They begin to lose accuracy in reporting on television as it functions in their environment, and they fall off completely with radio. Media research shows that only 2 percent of the population are consciously aware of radio as a vital source of information in their lives—about the same percentage who, when questioned, report *air* as one of the ingredients they consume in life. A few statistics suggest at least the scope of our involvement with radio: There are 320 million radios in the United States. The average household has 4.9 sets. Eighty million cars are equipped with radios. We spend over two hundred million dollars each year on transistor radio batteries.

People don't *remember* radio as a source of information because they do not consciously *listen* to it. Rather, they bathe in it and sit in it. Just as we are not conscious of breathing, we

are not actively aware of radio-mediated sound in our environment. Yet we are deeply involved with radio, and we are strongly affected by radio programming that allows us to participate. Recent attitude-change research has shown that the most favorable condition for affecting someone's attitude involves a source the listener depends on or believes in, and yet one he does not actively or critically attend. Thus radio is an ideal medium for affecting attitudes through evoked recall communication.

Television serves a similar function as radio for many people, at certain times of day. Many housewives use the afternoon soap operas as a *surround* for ironing or preparing meals. And many teen-agers do their homework in a Rowan and Martin surround. Common sense would suggest that this is a very conducive environment for communication. Participation is deep, and a listener or viewer uses the medium as a companion. Yet some advertisers are wary of the growing use of electronic media as environmental surround. One advertising executive put it this way:

> Background listeners are those who really don't listen at all, but regard radio as a pleasant accompaniment to whatever they're doing. . . . The more foreground listeners radio can deliver, the better we like it. We want alert, attentive listeners—juices flowing, money out, ready to run down to the corner drugstore.

When foreground radio becomes cluttered, it moves to the background of our attention. However, if background radio contains stimuli related to a listener's life (e.g., if it mentions his name), it becomes foreground again. Advertisers have used media only as a means of putting things into people, not as a means of evoking what is already in the listener. The background listener, or the passive viewer, has a sympathetic relation to his electronic environment. Further, he has a lifetime of experiences stored within him. A commercial can provide the stimuli to regenerate those experiences, bring them into the

This photograph is cluttered with signs for a general observer, but not someone looking for Fifty-seventh Street.

foreground, and associate them with a product. This form of learning is harder to reject since there is no explicit message bombarding the listener. Also, the viewer or listener is more likely to retain the effects of the commercial since he does not have to remember anything. If the commercial is successful, it builds an association between the product and meaningful experiences in real life that is permanently stored and available for recall in purchasing situations.

CONSUMERISM

Advertisers could have complete control over the attacks directed against them by consumer groups. However, the advertisers' focus on product *claims* prevents them from exercising this control.

Consumerism arose as a mass movement when public television exposed the commercial environment. When commercial TV was the only form of programming available, the public accepted it as synonymous with *television*. Only a relatively few people were acquainted with British or Canadian television, and therefore knew that the U.S. system was only one alternative. With public television, more people became aware that there are various television environments, and began to see the unique characteristics of commercial TV. NET, PBS, and various cable programming enabled us to step out of the commercial TV environment and see the pollution generated by certain advertising.

Consumerism is an antipollution drive in relation to the toxic areas of advertising. As such, it is *a reactive form of behavior*. Consumer groups utilize the Fairness Doctrine, equal time provisions, and other FCC laws that allow them to *respond* to some action that has taken place on the public airways. This reactive behavior is conditioned by the advertiser's output. Advertisers, therefore, can control the actions of consumer groups by carefully designing their own output. How-

USP=INCREDIBILITY

A major U.S. company that (1) states privately that there is absolutely no difference between their product and their competitors', and (2) finds no correlation between their advertising and *sales*, nonetheless bases their advertising on promoting a unique selling proposition:

> We believe in stressing unique product benefits. While most of
> our competitors' product contain _____, the _____ image be-
> longs to us. Our advertising has successfully developed an aware-
> ness of this product claim, even though it is an intangible.

ever, at the moment, advertisers view consumerism as something *they* should react against.

The advertising community will not control consumer groups
as long as the advertisers insist on making *claims* for products.
Advertisers are locked into this dangerous position because
they still hold onto the golden rule of USP; that is, they seek
to create a Unique Selling Proposition for their product.

This leads them to make claims about a product that are unreal, and therefore provides ammunition for consumer reaction
to those claims.

If one were to study a product's real meaning and value to
people, and use advertising to resonate with the experiences a
person has in relation to a product, it would not only create
the most effective advertising, it would disarm consumer
groups. FCC or FTC rules cannot be invoked against advertising that makes no false claims.

A manufacturer directly controls two of the three elements
affecting his company, and he can strongly influence the third.
The first factor is his product, and the second is paid media
(advertising). The third element, nonpaid media (word of
mouth, news, public attitudes, consumer groups' reactions,
etc.), can be conditioned by the second. Nonpaid media reacts
to, and is conditioned by, paid media. So in designing paid
media that resonates with the way a product relates to society,
and with the real needs and product values as people experience them, a manufacturer can generate positive feedback that
supports the advertising effort and achieves the desired behavioral effect of selling a product.

The Inside of the Outside

It has become popular to speak of political candidates as products that can be sold like soap, or formless creatures who need an *image* created for them by media specialists. Joe McGinnis, among others, has fostered a public interest in *image makers* and attributed almost magical powers to the tricks of their trade (*The Selling of the President, 1968*, Trident Press, 1969). Despite the critical tone of articles about them, image makers enjoy reading about the power they command, a power that has as much substance as the images they create.

Image makers concern themselves with makeup, lighting, camera angles, wardrobe, visual backgrounds, etc., or how a candidate *looks* to a viewer. His outside appearance constitutes his image. But this represents a serious misunderstanding of how television functions in relation to our senses.

The image makers follow a classic pattern of using an older medium (film) as the content of a new medium (TV). We have all witnessed this process many times. Telephone communication was filled with "telegrams." Print was filled with

talk. Movies were based on books, plays, and scripts. Television was filled with movies. Records were filled with perform-ances, and radio was filled with records. Even today, many of these media are used in the old way. However, the physical and structural characteristics of media exert greater control over our ideas and institutions than the content we receive from them. Media extend our senses into the world about us and structure our ways of learning, understanding, and com-municating. Also, the introduction of a new medium may up-set our sensory balance, thereby creating a new awareness of the world and new codes through which communication is structured. It is futile to employ television and radio in a political campaign as an extension of print or film. Television and radio are received differently from film or print. Our senses expect electronically mediated information to be organized in a particular way, and our brain applies different patterns in making sense of these data.

The "image people" work with concepts like *charismatic, handsome, youthful,* etc. And they strive to keep their candi-

date *moving*—through shopping centers, old-age homes, schools, etc. They utilize visual information on television to communicate this image. Television is thus conceptualized as a vehicle for bringing the voters to the candidate, where they can see and experience his glorious image.

I believe it is far more important to understand and affect the inner feelings of a voter in relation to a political candidate than to package an image that voters tend not to believe anyway. It would be more correct to say that the goal of a media adviser is to tie up the voter and deliver him to the candidate. So it is really the *voter* who is packaged by media, not the candidate. The voter is surrounded by media and dependent on it in his everyday functioning. The stimuli a candidate uses on the media thus surround the voter. They are part of his environment, his packaging.

A CANDIDATE'S RELATION TO HIS AUDIENCE

In assessing the reactions of voters to candidates on television, it becomes very clear that a person sitting in his home watching a political figure on his TV set four or five feet away wants to feel that the candidate is talking to him. A politician who typically speaks to large audiences, in a grandiose style, must adjust his speech scale for television or radio. Though he may be part of an audience totaling ten or twenty million people, a TV viewer experiences the candidate as someone speaking in his home to one, two, or maybe five people gathered around the set.

Any situation in which a politician is filmed may potentially find its way to the television viewer or the radio listener. Thus a politician on the street, shouting over the volume of traffic to fifty or a hundred people, must understand that a home audience of two or three million listening to him that

evening will be put off by his shouting. The home viewer's ear is, in effect, only four or five feet away from the politician's mouth. And there are no diesel trucks or air hammers in his living room.

When I work with a candidate, I encourage him to speak to small groups or single individuals on the street, so the personal quality of his voice will fulfill the expectations of a single person or small group listening to him on TV news programs. And when I record a candidate for radio or TV spots, I sit next to him and ask him to talk to me, not the microphone. If he sounds like he is reading from a script or begins talking to the mike, I interrupt and say, "You know, I don't feel you're talking to me." Many politicians in a recording situation will talk either to an imaginary vast audience spread across a wide geographic area, or *on behalf of themselves,* i.e., as if their position had been challenged by a reporter and they were defending it. A home listener is not interested in a politician who formally expresses a position. To the average voter, expressing-a-position-talk is what government officials do when they want to cover up something. A voter wants the candidate to talk *to* him, not *at* him; to use the medium not as a large public *address* system, but rather as a private *undress* system. Furthermore, many politicians tend to organize their thoughts for a home listener the way they might for a group of lawyers. But the logic of the positions they try to develop fails to impress the typical voter, who has one thought in the back of his mind whenever he listens to a politician: "How do I *feel* about him?"

Traditionally, successful politicians are usually quite effective in tuning their speech for a face-to-face audience. They learn to interpret very subtle feedback from a crowd and adjust their style to maximize the impact. However, when they have to speak to a radio or TV home audience (non-face-to-face), they often give a mechanical rendering of their feelings. Rather than adjust for a more intimate relation to the listener, they project for a larger audience.

When a politician is both speaking to a large face-to-face audience and being broadcast on radio, it would be wise to insure that his talk is properly framed for the home listeners, who may number in the millions. Simultaneously, he must affect the large public audience and the private home listener.

There are two possible solutions to this problem. The first solution is not yet possible in the United States, but it is used by Russian politicians. The largest convention hall in Moscow has several thousand seats. Each seat is equipped with its own speaker. Thus, a politician addressing a large public audience in the convention hall, while simultaneously speaking on radio or TV, can speak as if he were in the personal space zone of each listener. The convention hall listener and the home listener have approximately the same distance relation to the speaker. Any comparable American convention hall utilizes several large speakers to amplify a voice, not individual speakers at each seat. Thus, someone sitting in the audience may be twenty, thirty, or one hundred feet from a source of amplified sound, while the home listener is only three or four feet from the speaker's mouth.

A practical solution to this problem for an American politician is to address the large public audience the way he normally would, and use an announcer to *frame* his speech for the home listener. At the beginning and end, and at appropriate times during the speech, an announcer can remind the home listener, "We are listening to Senator Jones address the United Auto Workers Convention." In this way, the home listener changes his expectations of the candidate. Senator Jones is no longer talking to him. Rather, he is overhearing Senator Jones speak to the convention. Proper framing of the candidate is absolutely essential when a small piece of a public address is to be extracted for use in a political spot. Unless the home listener is told that the candidate was speaking to a large crowd when the segment was recorded, he will think the candidate is shouting at him. One example of misframing I remember, occurred in a spot for the late Adlai Stevenson. The

On an interview program, a political figure may find himself speaking simultaneously to the host in the studio, a reporter in another city, and to home listeners.

commercial opened with the announcer's voice, "Adlai Stevenson will now speak to you about his views on foreign aid." This was followed by a recorded segment of Stevenson speaking to a huge crowd.

To some degree, a candidate frames his own speech. He tells us that he regards the listener as a member of a large audience in a phrase such as, "My fellow Americans across this great land of ours . . ." And he frames a personal, one-to-one relation in a phrase such as, "Good evening, I appreciate the opportunity to come into your home tonight." Of course, tone of voice can support or contradict either of these frames.

It is much more important for a voter to feel a candidate than to see him. Despite all the myths to the contrary, a candidate's physical appearance alone does not win him many votes. But looks can lose votes. Generally, candidates tend to *look* dishonest, but *sound* honest. This visual handicap is magnified by the fact that most situations where a voter is likely to see the candidate are detrimental to his visual presentation of self. Television in particular is very difficult to structure for effective visual communication of a candidate. The candidate typically has no feeling of who is looking at him; he does not know which camera is on; and the lighting often puts him in a spotlight situation, not an interpersonal encounter. For these and other reasons, I tend to use the candidate much more on radio than on television.

TASK-ORIENTATION

It is often argued that TV *wears out* a candidate. This is generally true, but only because most political advertisers use a *campaign* approach (in the old product advertising sense) in creating and running TV spots. They make only a few commercials, weeks or months in advance of showing them on TV, and run them over and over. Since the commercials are produced so far in advance, they can only touch on general problems, not specific issues of the day. And since the public hears a candidate say the same irrelevant thing over and over, they get tired of him very quickly. A listener does not want to hear a candidate frozen on film saying the same thing. He expects the candidate to tell him something new all the time. He wonders why the candidate cannot speak to him "live." Videotape, combined with a task-orientation approach, can satisfy the public's demand for a fresh candidate. Videotape commercials can be assembled in hours instead of days, and a producer can create a number of spots on issues of immediate relevance, with minimal cost.

There are, of course, certain themes and issues that may be central to an election. Commercials dealing with these problems can be repeated. However, they should be works of art, which grows with multiple viewings. This all but eliminates a simple *candidate-talking* format. In its place, a symbolic approach counterpointing auditory and visual information is more likely to stand up. If a voter is going to see the commercial several times, he should be able to get more into it—and more out of it—each time he experiences it.

"Candidate *wear-out*" can take two forms: saturation *wear-out* from too much exposure of the candidate, and "fuse blow-out." Mario Procaccino, a candidate for mayor of New York City a while ago, blew out the receptivity fuses of people listening to him on radio, or listening and viewing on television. He was hotter than our personal media fuses could take. Every appearance on TV was like a performance before twenty thousand people at Madison Square Garden, without a microphone. He should be advised to run for mayor of a city like Havana or Saigon, where people generally watch TV in public, some distance from the set.

Important announcements by a candidate (e.g., that he is running for office) present special media problems. The broadcaster may cut a twenty-minute speech to one minute for the evening news. His message is not only cut to 5 percent of its original length, it is edited by someone who does not have the candidate's interests in mind. It makes sense, therefore, to use a forty-five-to-fifty-second speech when announcing something important. This way the speech will be covered in its entirety on the evening news. And the candidate, not the media, will be structuring how his position is presented to the public. Also, it recognizes the importance of electronic media. The home audience will no longer be given secondary status to the live public audience. At the same time people in the live audience need not be disappointed by his short speech. A new format can be developed for such occasions in which famous personalities and other politicians can supplement the program, with the candidate topping the bill.

My suggestion runs directly against the advice of many who say that political speeches and commercials should be longer.

Somehow, these people feel that a politician can more easily lie in ten seconds than in five minutes or one hour. However, I remember back in the thirties when radio was hailed as a means to shorten the long-windedness of politicians. At that time people felt that politicians had developed a special way of deceiving the public through long circumlocutions. Radio was perceived as beneficial to the electorate since it would force politicians to speak to the point and avoid unnecessary platitudes or bombast.

I do not feel that Eisenhower needed five minutes to say, "If elected, I will go to Korea." Similarly, Johnson did not require five minutes to announce that he would not seek reelection in 1968. Yet both these statements were quite clear, meaningful, and *truthful*. Time has nothing to do with clarity, truthfulness, or honesty. One can be clear or unclear, truthful or dishonest, in twenty seconds or two hours.

Another fascinating media problem is the disclaimer at the end of political spots. All political commercials are required to have a legal label at the end, stating who paid for the message. Naturally, there is a conflict between the candidate's interest in communicating an effective political message and the government's requirement of a label. The intent of the disclaimer is to frame the spot as a paid, partisan message. The problem for a media specialist is to minimize the negative effects of the label (from the candidate's point of view) without violating the law. A solution I have employed for some time is to integrate the label as part of the spot, rather than let it stand as a tag pasted on at the end. The name of the committee that pays for the spot is arbitrary. However, the official title must be exactly duplicated in the disclaimer. Some people might use *Committee for the Election of Senator Jones*, or *Senator Jones Campaign Committee*. I have used the title, *A Lot of People Who Want Bob Jones in the Senate*. This legal committee title can then be integrated into the commercial by a phrase such as, "And that's why this message was brought to you by . . ."

See how the two versions might affect you:

(A)   Political spot ends . . .
      ANNOUNCER: "Paid for by the Senator Jones Campaign Com-
      mittee."
(B)   Political spot ends . . .
      ANNOUNCER: "And that's why this message was brought to
      you by a lot of people who want Bob Jones in the Senate."

The 1971 San Francisco Alioto mayoralty campaign illustrates a very important principle in media campaigning. In the
early part of the campaign we emphasized Alioto's personal
feelings about a wide range of social problems. These were
very low-key spots designed to show voters that he was a man
of deep feelings. Later in the campaign our spots became
highly competitive: counterpointing Alioto's specific stand on
an issue with other candidates; building up his record and
attacking the record of other candidates; and asking the voter
to support him. We tried to give the voter concrete reasons
why he should vote for Alioto, and motivate him to perform
a specific act of behavior: pulling the Alioto lever in the voting
booth. This same kind of commercial would have been all
wrong at the beginning of the campaign. If we tell someone
why he should vote for a candidate and ask him to do so,
seven or eight weeks before the election, we are asking him to
perform the impossible. He cannot vote until election day.

In the early part of a campaign we simply want the voter to
think about the candidate and the issues. As the campaign
proceeds, we can focus on specifics, such as why someone
should support the candidate or why a given problem is important to the voter. Only in the last weeks should we ask
voters to come out for what Joe Napolitan calls the *one-day
sale*. In this way we do not create frustration in a potential
voter.

RESONANCE IN POLITICAL ADVERTISING

People tend to read ads for products they already own. The function of political advertising, then, may be characterized as organizing or confirming the feelings of two groups who already own (or believe in) many of the products (approaches to solving problems) a candidate is selling. The first group is the campaign workers and people who are planning to vote for the candidate. Their attitude can be reinforced by political advertising. The second group consists of those people who share certain of the candidate's feelings about social problems. Advertising can reveal the candidate's feelings to those who inherently share these beliefs. The realization of an identity between their feelings and the candidate's can provide a strong motivation to vote for the candidate. (We should not overlook the fact that a voter has *four* ways to vote: for or against either two candidates.)

It is very hard to change fixed beliefs. Hence, political advertising is not likely to change strongly held attitudes or convince a conservative Republican to vote for a liberal Democrat. However, most political decisions result from an interaction of many feelings and attitudes, often covering a wide spectrum of social beliefs. For example, there are many people who express a generally negative attitude about a candidate, but agree with many of the positions he expresses. One such individual might be someone who traditionally votes for party X but shares party Y's feeling that the economy can be strengthened. If you can evoke these feelings deeply, you may be able to change his overt voting behavior. Traditionalists in political science call this person a ticket splitter.

Television is an ideal medium for surfacing feelings voters already have, and giving these feelings a direction by providing stimuli that may evoke the desired behavior. The "newsreel" commercial, which shows a candidate moving about and talking to people, is not very effective for this purpose. I believe television spots function well as electronic posters for a candidate; i.e., they create auditory and visual stimuli that can evoke a voter's deeply held feelings. Indeed, the best political commercials are similar to Rorschach patterns. They do not tell the viewer anything. They surface his feelings and provide a context for him to express these feelings.

The real question in political advertising is *how to surround the voter with the proper auditory and visual stimuli to evoke the reaction you want for him,* i.e., *his voting for a specific candidate.*

A commercial I created for President Johnson in 1964 illustrates my point. The spot shows a little girl in a field counting petals on a daisy. As her count reaches ten, the visual motion is frozen and the viewer hears a countdown. When the countdown reaches zero, we see a nuclear explosion and hear President Johnson say, "These are the stakes, to make a world in which all God's children can live, or to go into the darkness. Either we must love each other or we must die." As the screen goes to black at the end, white lettering appears stating, "on November 3rd, Vote for President Johnson."

The *Daisy* spot was shown only once, on "Monday Night at the Movies," but it created a huge controversy. Many people, especially the Republicans, shouted that the spot accused Senator Goldwater of being trigger-happy. But *nowhere in the spot is Goldwater mentioned.* There is not even an indirect reference to Goldwater. Indeed, someone unfamiliar with the political climate in 1964 and viewing the spot today will not perceive any allusion at all to Goldwater. Then why did it bring such a reaction in 1964? Well, Senator Goldwater had stated previously that he supported the use of tactical atomic weapons. The commercial *evoked* a deep feeling in many people that Goldwater might actually use nuclear weapons. This mistrust was not in the *Daisy* spot. It was in the people who viewed the commercial. The stimuli of the film and sound evoked these feelings and allowed people to express what they inherently believed. Even today, when people try to remember the *Daisy* spot, they recall their feelings, not the actual con-

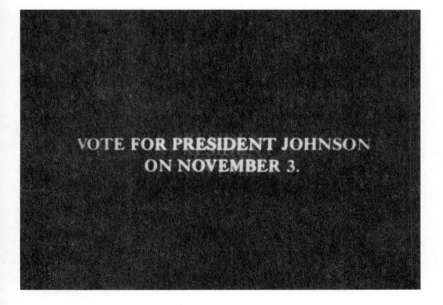

tent of the commercial—for example, in the following New York *Times* article, the writer actually quotes something that was never in the commercial:

> In 1964, the Democrats demolished Goldwater with a simple one-shot television spot. A little girl gently picking daisies moved happily across an open field. Suddenly, a mushroom cloud filled the air and the announcer asked sternly: "Whose finger do you want on the trigger?"
>
> Ted Venetoulis
> New York *Times*
> May 22, 1972, p. 35

Probably the smartest thing Goldwater could have done at the time was to agree with the attitude of the commercial and offer to help pay for running it. This would have undercut the sensational effect of it and possibly won him many votes.

Political advertising involves tuning in on attitudes and beliefs of the voter and then affecting these attitudes with the proper auditory and visual stimuli. If our research shows that most people feel one vice presidential candidate is clearly superior, we do not have to hit him over the head with this information in order to make it work for us. We might simply list their names on a card and ask, "Who is your choice to be a heartbeat away from the presidency?" In this way, you surface attitudes (held by many) that can produce the desired effect. Commercials that attempt to *tell* the listener something are inherently not as effective as those that attach to something that is already in him. We are not concerned with getting things *across* to people as much as *out* of people. Electronic media are particularly effective tools in this regard because they provide us with direct access to people's minds.

In situations where voters do not share the same feelings or have divergent views on a subject, we must design stimuli that will be meaningful to the different groups within the audience, at the same time. For example, in a gubernatorial race we were faced with a large bloc of public school teachers

who might vote for the candidate if he promised to increase their pay. At the same time, the general public objected to an increase in teachers' salaries, feeling that the quality of teaching was too low to merit higher wages. One solution to this conflict might involve having the candidate promise to "upgrade teachers." The teachers could interpret this as *upgrade salary*, while the general public might hear it as *upgrade quality*.

PAID AND NONPAID MEDIA

A major problem of political candidates is to structure the effects of nonpaid media, such as news, word of mouth, editorials, etc. A candidate gets more free time in a campaign than paid time. In my work I try to use paid media (political spots) to put nonpaid media in context. I do not see them as unrelated to each other. If there is a lot of news about the candidate, and you do not feel it is accurately framed by the newscaster, station, or newspaper, you can put it in a proper frame by use of paid media.

Let me cite an example outside the area of political campaigning. Con Edison, a large eastern power utility, is constantly receiving bad press because of power failures. However, the same people who hear this news have also heard, at other times, that Con Edison's repeated attempts to build new plants are rejected by the Public Service Commission because of objections by various groups. Con Edison could put those two pieces of news together in paid spots and thereby give the power failure a proper context, a reason for happen-

---

An example of how paid media can affect future nonpaid media occurred in the 1972 Ogden Reid campaign. Here, we used paid media to create a controversy.

"Hello, I'm Ogden Reid and I'm running for re-election to Congress from Westchester. I'm demanding a *public* explanation from the Public Service Commission. Mr. Swidler, how can you justify handing the telephone company a 361-million-dollar increase and other special favors, at the expense of the New York phone user? Sure, the telephone company has problems modernizing and making ends meet, but so do people. When are you going to start working for the public?"

Positive and negative reactions to this spot were covered by the press, at no cost to the candidate. All reactions worked for the candidate. For example, Jack Anderson reported that two phone company executives contributed money to Reid's opponent after seeing the spot. That money and their two votes were a small price to pay for the free coverage by Anderson—from which people could feel that Reid was a defender of the public interest.

ing. Later, when a person hears of a new power failure, he is likely to associate it with news of plants being rejected. Paid media would have taught him to attach two pieces of information from his environment. In this way, Con Edison can make an ally, rather than an enemy, of the public.

Paid media can also be used to introduce new information into the environment, for later recall. An incumbent can take a position on a given problem and use paid media to convey his stance to the public. Later, when running for re-election, he can recall this position in his advertising. He can use the public's earlier experience of him as support in his current campaign. Similarly, a nonofficeholder can use paid media before the campaign to communicate his position on a problem that is currently very important. He thus establishes himself as an authority on the problem or a champion of a cause. This can be recalled later when he announces his candidacy.

Within a campaign, we can utilize people's experience by integrating early spots into later spots. For this reason, some of my commercials near the end of a campaign are often a montage of the first ones. Usually I can evoke people's full experience of the early commercials by using bits and pieces of them, properly designed. This makes use of a principle in perception, that people most readily understand things they have seen and heard before. This also prevents the negative effects of hearing the same thing over and over again.

I also apply this principle in using a candidate's name. It is a standard rule of mine that whenever a candidate's name appears in print, either in a newspaper ad or as graphics in a TV spot, it should look exactly as it will in the voting booth. This includes both the formal name and the type face.

RESEARCH AS X RAY

Most advertising research investigates whether people understand the message told by a commercial, and if they retain it. Good political research seeks out attitudes in the environment and then judges a political spot by the way it affects these attitudes. I was introduced to this approach by Joseph Napolitan, whom I regard as the best political campaign strategist in the world. Napolitan has taught me the value of task-orientation in political and product advertising. Commercials must enter a complex world of attitudes and behavior. A political spot has meaning only to the extent that it affects behavior at the voting end. There is no way you can test a commercial in isolation to see how it will function. A political spot is broadcast into an environment rich with interaction: People are talking to friends about a candidate, reading and watching news, listening to other candidates' spots, etc. This is where a commercial must function, not in a theater testing environment. A person does not listen to a political spot in isolation and then decide whom he will support, based on this single input. Therefore, the commercials must function as part of the environment. They must interact with all the elements present in a person's environment and produce the desired behavioral effect. The people listening are actually part of the content of any commercial. Their feelings and beliefs interact with the commercial stimuli in creating any attitudinal changes.

Curiously, although I have created thousands of spots for commercial products, advertising agency research never provided me with information I could use in designing a commercial. Napolitan's task-oriented research carefully analyzes a candidate's problems and identifies for me those problems that can best be solved through electronic media. It works as an X ray for me. I will then create a commercial for each specific problem. Most political advertising, especially agency spots, works on a "let's think of some good ideas for commercials" principle. However, we always use research as a rudder for creating commercials, and this produces very different results.

After we learn the specific problem we want to solve and the environment our spot must function in, we can use media as stimuli, not content. This enables us to utilize our audience as a work force that our paid media affects, rather than as a target that our paid media must hit.

The political poll is a way to measure attitudes and concerns of people in the environment. It can provide raw data that are valuable only to someone who can analyze it honestly and critically. As an X ray, it is a great tool if it is read correctly. For instance, we often deal with a LOP factor—that is, a favorable response on a poll often means that the candidate is the Least Objectionable Politician. "Politician" is a negative word and tends to group with others, like "landlord," "tax collector," "meter maid," "salesman," etc., in the public's ear. If one accepts this view, the logical task of the media specialist is to make his candidate the least objectionable politician in the race. Many presidential campaigns have been organized with this specific task as the major goal.

Research also reveals that issues are relatively unimportant. As long as pollsters ask voters whether the economy, defense spending, or transportation deserves the most attention, we can obtain only a list of the relative importance among various issues. But if issue-oriented questions are mixed with inquiries about personal qualities of the candidates in a single poll question, the relative unimportance of issues is revealed in a startling way. The following is the result of a poll taken in 1969 and 1970 by Michael Rowan in several states.

QUESTION:* If you were to see a TV program about a candidate running for governor, what would you like to know or feel about him after seeing it?
Answers broke down this way:

That he is honest, a man of conviction	47%
That he is a hard worker	27%
That he is an understanding, compassionate man	14%
That he is a capable, qualified person	9%
That he is a good person, warm	7%
That he is a leader, bold	5%
That he is a bright, intelligent man	4%
That he is a man who perceives the vital issues	3%
No response	8%

No one should interpret this as meaning that people are not concerned about issues. All our research reveals that people are *consumed* by issues. The point here is that when it comes time to choose the person to be elected, voters are looking for the man best capable of dealing with the issues. Most of the problems he will face in office do not arise until after the election. Issues in the campaign are typically a list of past problems. Kevin White, mayor of Boston, put this quite well: .

---

* The question was open-ended; that is, the nine groups of responses were not offered by the interviewer, they were coded after-the-fact and came directly and spontaneously from the respondents.

I had no way of knowing that two months after I took office as mayor of Boston, that the biggest problem I would face would be getting fuel oil into the city to keep the people warm. That's not the kind of thing you can anticipate. What you need in office is a man who can cope with situations as they arise, situations that no one ever thought of.

Kevin White
Personal recording

It is personal qualities like honesty or integrity that tell a voter whether the candidate will be able to handle problems when they arise in the future. Understanding this, the task of a media specialist is not to reveal a candidate's stand on issues, so much as to help communicate those personal qualities of a candidate that are likely to win votes.

The campaign slogan, a carry-over of print's historical role in political campaigns, has little relevance in task-oriented political advertising. Print fostered a long-range *program* approach to campaigning. The time lead needed in organizing, producing, and distributing printed materials (e.g., pamphlets, billboard ads, posters, etc.) required a great deal of guesswork about the problems that would emerge during the campaign. The slogan was an attempt to focus on a central, overriding issue that would serve as a theme for the entire campaign.

The task-oriented use of electronic media enables the candidate to deal with campaign problems on a fire-fighting or guerrilla warfare basis—to tune media to needs (or calculate feedback), to go deep rather than broad. On a given day people may feel that the candidate is antilabor (e.g., the day after the president of the United Auto Workers attacked him in a speech), or that car safety is the most important issue facing the country (e.g., the day after General Motors announces it is recalling one million cars to correct defects). The long-range *program* campaign cannot deal with these specific problems that arise on a day-to-day basis. A task-oriented campaign can create, overnight, a commercial that relates to a problem that has just arisen. For example, I received a call one afternoon from Joe Napolitan in Massachusetts. A problem had just come up and he wanted a spot to handle it immediately. I designed a commercial, called our announcer (Bob Landers) in Los Angeles, who had the recorded material on a plane to me in hours; I edited the material and made several copies that evening, and it was on the air the following morning. The quicker we respond to a problem, the greater are our chances of achieving a desired effect. Also, this utilizes a principle McLuhan described to me some time ago: "Instant information creates involvement in depth."

A task-oriented approach can also be applied to buying radio and TV time. It is important that we reach the specific audience for whom the spot will be most relevant. Task-oriented time buying involves a careful analysis of the people who listen to radio or watch TV at various times. Time buying in most advertising agencies is detached. They purchase air time for a candidate's media the same way regular product time is bought, *on a bargain basis*. Packages of air time are purchased with little or no thought given to the people who may be reached by a specific political spot.

Time buys should be tuned to specific problems. The first time I worked with Ruth Jones, an independent time buyer who has worked on many of our campaigns, I was delightfully shocked when she asked to hear the spots before she bought air time for them. It may seem obvious that a time buyer should do this, but in all my years of creating commercials for products, no agency time buyer ever discussed the commercials with me to determine how we could best reach those people the spot would affect.

There are a host of considerations in time buying. An afternoon radio program with light music will attract more older people than a late-night rock program, and is therefore a better environment for placing a spot about Social Security. However, advertisers can buy time with a good deal more sophistication than simply correlating the demographic characteristics of a program's audience with the subject matter in a given spot. Advertisers can pinpoint the hours when people are driving to and from work in their cars (and the programs drivers listen to most), and affect them with the sound they sit in. These spots can be designed for car listening. The physical characteristics of sound can be equalized to maximize its impact in a car environment. Similarly, the advertiser can alter the characteristics of a spot if he knows it will be heard by people primarily in kitchens, or living rooms, or outdoors, or any other environment. I designed commercials in a gubernatorial race specifically for beach listening. The spots were played on a Labor Day weekend during the afternoon. We knew that 70 percent of the people listening to radio at this time would be at the beach.

By directing our spots toward a highly selected local audience, it is often possible to give the feeling of a national campaign. For example, we can determine the radio stations congressmen and senators listen to in Washington, D.C., at what hours, and saturate those media environments with our spots. In this way, a relatively unknown person (or issue) may become a national political figure (or national issue) overnight. (Similarly, we have found that advertising exclusively on the op ed page of the New York *Times* may generate the feeling of a national campaign in the corporate environment.)

Task-oriented time buying also permits us to match or counterpoint the mood of the commercial with the mood of the person listening to our spot. For example, the mood of a person listening to radio in the morning, as opposed to the afternoon or evening will be quite different. Radio and television serve different functions at different times of day. The design of a political spot should relate to the way it will be used in a person's life. If we were in a person's home at each of these times of day, we would vary the way we speak to him, in order to heighten the effect of what we say. A political spot should function in the same way. It should speak to a person in a way that reaches him.

MUNICATION AND COMMUNICATION

Nonpaid media, such as news, and paid political media are disseminated to a vast audience, at great speed, with extraordinary efficiency. However, the flow of information is essentially in one direction. The public cannot easily feed back their opinions, suggestions, and objections. The President can at any moment reach the entire nation via television. But a member of the public cannot reach him, except through an inefficient letter or a vote once every four years. This is not a healthy situation in a *participatory* democracy.

Rather than condemn electronic media as corrupting forces in politics (a futile, as well as an incorrect position), I suggest that we have not yet even begun to explore the potential of electronic media in creating two-way political communication. The two-way potential of cable networks, and the current availability of telephone as a feedback line to radio or TV, establish a realistic basis for town meetings that include an entire city, state, or even the nation. Similarly, we can use two-way cable or the telephone to instantly poll vast segments of the population on important problems.

Electronic communication does not signal the end of democracy. Rather, it offers the potential of genuine democracy in a nation of over two hundred million people.

If Booth Tarkington were to write *Seventeen* today, he would have to call it *8½*.

A child growing up in our culture a hundred years ago would most likely learn about a kangaroo from books. He would necessarily have to read in order to acquire this knowledge, and many things about a kangaroo would not be easily learned, e.g., how it jumps. Print learning required a great deal of effort by the child for relatively little knowledge input.

When film became available as a learning tool, a child could learn about the kangaroo or an Eskimo or the Amazon River at a younger age—before he learned how to read. Also, a wider range of knowledge could be acquired with less effort, e.g., any behavior involving motion. However, film was not an everyday experience for the child. He went to the movies once or twice a week, at most.

With the wide dissemination of television sets, all children in our culture grow up in a highly saturated information environment. At age two or three, a child can imitate a kangaroo

jump, or describe how men walk on the Moon. When the meteorologist for a New York TV station was asked why the six o'clock weather reports are more technical than the eleven o'clock reports, he responded, "Because the early show is seen by more kids. They understand the scientific gadgets and words better than their elders." A child today has a more sophisticated knowledge of a much larger world at a much younger age.

Electronic media provide the same information to adults and children. When books provided most information about events outside our immediate experience, a child was *sheltered* from knowledge. Society regulated what children learned and the pace at which they learned. Today, electronically mediated information is equally available to all age groups. As a result, the generation gap has disappeared. It is the *absence* of such an information gap that causes much of the friction we are

A four-year-old who was never taught how to hold a guitar assumed this stance when handed one.

experiencing. The two groups, adults and children, are encountering each other more directly than ever before. These encounters are often painful because each group finds a different meaning in the event, based on the different sensory patterns each applies to experience.

Young people's media involvement not only provides them with more information, and experiences commonly shared with everyone in the society than earlier generations, it also restructures their patterns of reacting, feeling, and thinking. Today's child is a scanner. His experience with electronic media has

Print-oriented people bring their bias to the new media. Here, David Rockefeller and his board of directors line up to hear the chief.

taught him to scan life the way his eye scans a television set or his ears scan auditory signals from a radio or stereo speaker. The child's mode of thinking is now in sync with his mode of perceiving. There is no longer a conflict between the way his senses pattern information and the way his brain organizes these sensory data to give meaning to experience. When print dominated our communication environment, men sought conceptual knowledge about the world. To achieve this, sensory information had to be translated into a linear, cognitive mode. In our electronic communication environment no translation is necessary. A young person perceives sensory information a millisecond at a time, and he experiences life as a continuous stream of fleeting, millisecond events. In this way of life, involvement has greater value for young people than conceptual knowledge about the world.

~~~~~~

SENSORY MISMATCH

I remember in my second year of teaching in a small Eskimo fish-
ing town of Alaska, the frustrations of a newly-arrived math teacher
who had the classroom next to mine. He claimed that he "couldn't
get through to the Eskimos" because of "deficiencies in hearing"—
and this, he explained, was the reason for his yelling, screaming,
and pounding on the blackboard day after day. After several
weeks of this he asked me the trouble and I told him about Eskimo
eyebrows.

Eskimos give sharp definition to yes, no, and maybe answers with
their face and eyebrows. He had come there expecting verbal feedback. When he .didn't get it, he assumed that it was because of
bad hearing among the Eskimos, so he raised his voice.

There is a saying in that part of Alaska that white people are
craziest when they first get to the village.

<div align="right">Michael Rowan
Personal memo</div>

~~~~~~

To someone with an old sensory orientation, this process
seems like a fragmentation of life, in which a person lives
only moment to moment with no sense of history, no connection to the past, and no goals for the future. But to someone
immersed in this scanning process, his experience of life is
totally in sync with his perception of the world around him.
His patterns of auditory and visual perception are in harmony
with his pattern of thinking.

How does a young person experience the world around him?
Well, if I show someone a still photograph of a scene, he can
perceive certain facts about the scene: what is there, its shape,
number, etc. If I take a motion picture of a scene, a viewer
can see which elements in the scene move and which do not,
and where the elements that move go. If I shoot a great deal
of footage over a period of time and run it at high speed, so
the action is speeded up, a viewer can begin to perceive pat-

terns of interaction: where things regularly go and where they do not regularly go, and the probability of various outcomes because of these interactions. The high speed of information reveals patterns to those who are open to the experience. Young people experience life in an accelerated way. The high speed of information in their lives reveals patterns of interaction very easily. They are not only more open to this process than older people, they seek it out.

In everyday encounters with young people, the educator often fails to recognize the differences between a student's use of his senses, and patterning of sensory information, and the teacher's own. Educators stress analytic, deductive reasoning, which conforms to the way they think, while students scan huge amounts of information in search of patterns. The educator would like his students to *understand fully* something they see or hear, and not miss any information. In an age of information overload this is a death warrant. The student must learn to scan to live. The educator's new job is to sharpen this skill so a student can efficiently process the vast quantities of information he experiences in life.

A RESONANCE APPROACH

A child enters the classroom today with the world stored in him. He possesses more information than any school could ever teach him. As a result, the education process has been reversed. Rather than cram new information into an *empty shell,* the school's function is to *order existing knowledge.* That is, to promote recall and feedback of the student's own experiences and involve him in the learning process—so he can best utilize the information stored within him.

In this situation, the teacher has a much more complex role. He is no longer a bricklayer, piling up pieces of knowledge in a student. Rather, he helps a student discover how building materials (the student's experiences outside the classroom) can be structured to serve the student's needs. The tools he designs for these education encounters should be devices that organize into a meaningful context the raw knowledge a student has accumulated from life. The teacher can make the student aware of that which he already knows, and understand its meaning for his social and intellectual growth.

Since the information stored within a child is patterned in a different way from previous generations, we are not going to reach him with new information patterned in the old print-based linear structure. And we are not going to evoke the information stored within him by using the old patterns. The media child demands participation and a sense of community with those who share the learning experience with him. The education process has to leave space, large chunks of space, to allow the child to participate. If the educator does not allow participation and anticipate a student's desire to feed back his own experience with the education input, our system will push the child out of the school entirely. Unfortunately, the present education establishment is more concerned with *filling time* than involving students. Both the tax structure that supports a school and internal demands placed on a teacher (e.g., submitting lesson plans) foster relentless, one-way munication from teacher to student. It is unthinkable, in the present education scheme, that a teacher plan a day when no one comes to school, but simply thinks about what they have learned or tries to apply it in their everyday life.

The media child enters school closely united to his fellow students by a common experience of the world, which results from their common use of media. He can fill in, or respond to, or resonate with a vast amount of information that he shares with others in the class. Also, children will make sense of new experiences by referring them to *common* previous experiences. This information common to all children who grow up with electronic media is the greatest teaching resource available to an educator, but he must know how to use it.

A teacher's classroom input can bring to mind those things

a student has seen or heard before, and place it in a new context that serves an educational purpose. From this perspective, television becomes a valuable *reading readiness* tool. The teacher can design reading materials that utilize a child's media experiences. These experiences are the same for all children in the classroom, and they can be known by the teacher before he or she ever meets the children.

Similarly, audio-visual materials can serve to organize other media learning, as well as provide new learning patterned to conform with a child's media experiences. They can recall events that every student has experienced (e.g., the Moon landing) and restructure them in an educational context. Thus auditory and visual material can serve as a recall mechanism, rather than as a transmission mechanism. They restructure what a student knows without telling him anything new.

Anything that has appeared on television and has been viewed by students can be reorganized both to recall the experience of viewing the material and to give it new meaning by virtue of its new structure. For example, the network footage of a news event such as a presidential campaign can be edited together and given a point of view. This can evoke the student's experience of these events at home, and allow him to participate in structuring the new point of view, organized by the teacher's editing of the material. Similarly, there is a wealth of educational material in old movies, apart from the typical use of films as a supplement to literature. The most accurate part of a Hollywood movie is the costuming and set design. The movie may distort beyond recognition the literary value or the facts about the historical event or social setting, but the scenery, costumes, tools, weapons, etc., are usually accurate in their depiction of the era. It remains a simple task for the educator to gather movie footage from several films about an era, edit it, and thus provide an involving account of the historical setting for a war, clothing styles in a rural community, or religious practices in puritanical New England.

Just as we can use paid political media (TV and radio spots) to structure the effect of nonpaid media (news, word of mouth, etc.), we can use the classroom experience to structure the effect of nonclassroom experiences. Television programming, for example, becomes a valuable education experience once a student learns to strip away the thin *content structure* that frames the behavior taking place. What we normally see, hear, and talk about in relation to a program (i.e., the story) is only 5 percent of what takes place. The underlying behavior (i.e., the nonacted behavior) occupies 95 percent of the program. A horse walking on "Bonanza" is not acting—it is the real behavior of a horse. Marcus Welby's *frown* in an *acted* situation nonetheless depicts a real facial movement. Even TV commercials show real behavior (e.g., they often show how a person talks when he knows precisely what he is going to say, but wants to give the feeling of spontaneity). A student can be taught to ask "what's going on" on TV, and *given permission* to look through the story veil to see the behavior taking place.

PRINT IN THE CLASSROOM

Strangely, we are in a better position to understand the function of print now that we are immersed in an electronic communication environment. Our capability of non-face-to-face auditory communication frees us from a dependence on writing to represent the spoken word in all non-face-to-face situations. As a result, we can for the first time study the relation between writing and speech. In today's environment, we have a choice of communication modes. When man depended on print for all non-face-to-face communication, he could not easily learn its inherent abilities. He had no alternative but to make it serve all communication needs.

The child entering school today is a member of an auditory-based culture. The written symbol merely *represents* speech for him. It does not replace speech as a vehicle for communicating important or lasting ideas. Nor does written grammar replace ordinary speech usage as an ideal structure for language. Prescriptive grammar is a set of rules for putting words on paper, not taking them off, or organizing spoken words that never touch paper. In addition, a child can more readily understand how writing structures meaning. He can perceive writing as a medium because it is only one of the forms available to him. A child's concept of self and his general view of the world are rooted in an auditory base, the structure of electronic communication. Writing tries to impose a more symbolic, abstract view of the world that is not as involving for the child as his auditory-based understanding of the world.

In testing, as well as in teaching, most educators are concerned primarily with print-related abilities. Slowness or lack of interest in reading is thought to denote a sluggish intellect. However, such a system cannot accurately measure the abilities of blind people, Australian Bushmen, or the average young American today, for each of these groups uses its senses differently than the print-oriented education establishment. In addition, the learning skills many educators try to develop in students hinder the students' understanding of electronically mediated communication.

Isolating one sense from all others calls for enormous training and self control and is probably never fully achieved. . . . A child learns to separate the senses when he learns, in class, to read silently. His legs twist, he bites his tongue, but by an enormous *tour de force* he learns to fragment his senses, to turn on one at a time and keep the others in neutral. And so he is indoctrinated into that literate world where readers seek silent solitude.

> Ted Carpenter
> *They Became What They Beheld*
> Outerbridge & Dienstfrey
> New York, 1970

Concentration, for example, is a valuable skill in reading but unimportant in electronic learning. Whereas a student must concentrate to block out unrelated sensory information while reading, his perceptual orchestration is geared by media experiences early in life to provide an open channel for electronically mediated communication. In reading, the ability to learn depends on the ability to concentrate. With electronic media, it is *openness* that counts. Openness permits auditory and visual stimuli more direct access to the brain. Moreover, someone who is taught to *concentrate* will fail to perceive many patterns of information conveyed by electronic stimuli.

A child does not have to read in order to acquire knowledge. This is not to argue that reading is an unimportant skill. However, it is no longer an essential skill that must be acquired before a child can grow intellectually. Schools might well adopt a task-orientation approach to reading skills. A child should learn to read when he needs to read, or when he wants to take a "literacy trip." With a task-orientation approach, the age at which a child learns to read may change. Reading will not be the first task a child encounters when he enters school. Also, he will learn to read material that relates to his life. One teacher in New Jersey applied this principle and achieved remarkable success in teaching high school dropouts to read. Instead of using elementary reading textbooks, he employed pornographic literature as source material. He was fired.

SPEECH AND WRITING

For most teachers, "standard American speech" means speech that imitates the written word. Of course, the function of a written phonetic code originally was to represent speech. Somehow this has been reversed by educators, who insist that students speak in the classroom the way they write. A child is taught that speech in all situations must be expressed according to the grammatical rules of print if it is to be considered

By and large those who have discussed communication have been concerned with the production of words and their *proper* usage. . . . Not only were these men literate but they were devoted to the perfection of literacy. It is scarcely surprising that they placed such a high evaluation upon reading and writing that they unconsciously conceived the spoken language to be a clumsy and imperfect derivation of the written. Such a position cannot possibly reveal that the written language is rather a special shorthand of the spoken.

> Ray Birdwhistell
> *Kinesics and Context*
> University of Pennsylvania Press
> Philadelphia, 1970, p. 67

correct. This is a grand illusion on the part of the education system, because spoken American English differs considerably from one situation to another, and rarely conforms to the written code. As soon as the teacher leaves school and tries to buy groceries at a supermarket, his speech pattern will deviate from talking in a classroom. Even a verbatim transcript of a teacher's own classroom speech is filled with grammatical errors, as it must be in order to communicate. We could not communicate effectively if we spoke the way we write.

The classroom can be used to help students understand how they talk in different contexts. No one ever explains to children that speech in a job interview, as opposed to speech at a party or speech in a railroad station, has to vary considerably, if a person is to function effectively in those environments. Indeed, many teachers would sharply dispute this. Yet there are people who move through life orally crippled because they have not learned how to talk in different situations. They talk to a mechanic in a garage the same way they talk to a minister, and wonder why they never get proper service for their car. Changing the way we talk in various situations does not mean that the *content* of speech is different. It simply recognizes the need to resonate with the past experiences and current expectations of a listener. In the same way, many teachers never accept the language of gestures or tone of voice in relation to the verbal content of speech.

The function of writing in the global village classroom is not very different from its original role. The written word is a way of representing speech communication in non-face-to-face situations. Poets have never lost sight of this relationship. Robert Frost, for example, argued that the written word is the servant of speech: "The ear is the only true writer and the only true reader. . . . sentence sounds are very definite entities. They're apprehended by the ear. They're gathered by the ear from the vernacular. The most original writer only catches them fresh from talk where they grow spontaneously." (Margaret B. Anderson, *Robert Frost and John Bartlett: The Record of a Friendship*, Holt, Rinehart & Winston, 1963.)

In order to develop a student's writing skills he should, first, be placed in an environment that is physically conducive to talking, and rich in the variety of speech that takes place. But if we examine the average classroom, we find it useless for developing the perceptual skills necessary to write well. In a typical classroom, the acoustic environment discourages speech communication. Any carpeted living room would be better. The difficulty a child might have listening in this setting is compounded by teachers who often turn their backs and write something on the blackboard while speaking. Classroom acoustics have also fostered a peculiar form of speech: teacher talk. Teacher talk generally consists of overvoicing or a booming quality, accompanied by sharp transitions in pitch and monosyllabic drawl to emphasize a word or syllable. Although teacher talk may help a teacher to be heard in a classroom, its communication value is very low. Like traffic cop talk and scolding mother talk, teacher talk limits a communication exchange and fosters one-way munication. The consequence is summarized by Camus, who said, "On the stage as in reality, the monologue precedes death."

A second prewriting skill involves the study of speech situations. Speech patterns may be related to a specific job, a social relationship, the physical environment, a psychological state of mind, etc. Experiencing an emotional event can have a distinct affect on the rhythm of one's speech. The announcer's voice after the Bobby Thomson home run demonstrates simply and dramatically how an event influences speech pattern. Conversely, speech pattern may evoke emotion. For example, in a gospel church the minister uses a rhythmic pattern in his speech to strike an emotional chord in the congregation and evoke feelings that will move the service in a particular direction. The interaction of physical environment with social relationship, or psychological state with job, may cause radical shifts in speech pattern within a very brief period. Erving Goffman (in *The Presentation of Self in Everyday Life,* Doubleday, 1959) touches on this point in a humorous way with his example of a seaman visiting his mother after a long voyage. The seaman, in Goffman's story, maintains all the correct civilities of talking to one's mother until he sits down at the dinner table. Here, the pattern of the event evokes the mannerisms he uses on the ship, and he asks his mother to "pass the _____ing butter." The intricate and complex elements present in speech situations must be *opened up* to the student as an important area of study underlying writing.

A third prewriting skill involves a study of the broad social and historic relationship between speech and technology. During the period when print dominated our communication environment, we could not perceive how typography and the mechanization of printing affected the spoken word. McLuhan points out that British upper-class speech imitated the sound of print. This characteristic of their voice was an instrument for establishing and maintaining class distinctions:

> There's a nice illustration of the effects of the written word on speech in Eliot's *Wasteland.* The clue comes from his use of the name Mrs. *Equitone.* You see, you mimic the effect of typography with the voice . . . equitone. The voices are close to printing because of the equality. The amount of variation in rhythm is slight compared to . . . well, you take Joyce's opening

of his recitation, "Well you know or haven't I told ya, every telling has a tale an that's the he and the she of it." Now this is non literate speech. The brogues of the world or dialects, Negro or otherwise, are not affected by print . . . no leveling off of nuance and pattern. But this Mrs. Equitone is really a very useful bit because the whole British upper class mimic with voice the world of printing. This puts the lower classes way down because they still retain many of the characteristics of pre-print in their voices. So the class structure in England is quite simply simulating print with the voice.

> Marshall McLuhan
> Personal recording

Today, we can hear voices that imitate machines. For example, a child using a teaching machine with a typing sound or computerized voice will imitate the staccato rhythm of the type or computer voice. In addition, technology fosters speech patterns in tune with the characteristics of a given medium. The difference between announcer styles on AM vs. FM is due, in part, to the differences between the physical characteristics of the two modes.

Writing can be viewed as a *translation* problem. How can the spoken word be translated into the written word and still retain meaning? For example, how does a particular writing instrument affect the way spoken words are recorded on paper? Ben Shahn argues that the *sound* of written words varies with the instrument used to put them on paper:

> I often wonder how many poets write in long hand. It really would be interesting to know. One might surmise that verse written to the staccato clack, clack of the typewriter might differ enormously from that written in the noiseless and rhythmic movements of the hand. Ogden Nash claims to have broken the sound barrier in his verse, but I wonder after all, was it he or was it the typewriter?

> Ben Shahn
> *Love and Joy About Letters*
> Grossman Publishers, 1963

How can a student write in order to retain the meaning of the *sound* of speech? And how can one put words on paper that must later be translated back into speech? Robert Frost discusses the first problem:

> The sound of sense is the abstract vitality of our speech. It is pure sound, pure form. One who concerns himself with it more than the subject is an artist. A sentence is a sound in itself on which other sounds called words, may be strung. You may string words together without a sentence sound just as you may tie clothes together by the sleeves and stretch them without a clothesline between two trees, but it is bad for the clothes.
>
> Anderson, *Robert Frost and John Bartlett*

Bob Marcato, a superb commercial announcer, talks about the second problem in relation to copy for a radio or TV spot:

> When you're working on the ear, you're working on sound. And once sound penetrates the ear, then you're working on the emotions of people. Now, do I have to *say* something to stir the emotions, or, shall I *sound* something to stir the emotions? Certain words require to be sounded, not said. "What's new? . . . Whatsnew?" The second "Whatsnew?" is slurred, but it is acceptable to you because it *sounds* right. Therefore, in commercial copy there are certain words, certain phrases that are not to be said, they are to be sounded.
>
> Bob Marcato
> Personal recording

If we use normal punctuation marks in written copy, it will be very difficult for someone to *sound* the words. Commas, semicolons, etc., are designed for the *written word*. An actor or oral reader presented with such copy will structure his speech like written grammar, not spoken words. There is clear need for a system of oral punctuation marks that will indicate what people do when they speak.

Similarly, many natural speech events cannot be transcribed

with grammatical punctuation. Spoken words that make complete sense when heard, are incongruous when transcribed with written punctuation marks. For example, one is hopelessly lost in trying to transcribe nonliterate speech with commas, colons, and periods. The following transcription employs normal punctuation marks for a speech segment that was spoken from an oral grammar base:

> He was a good kid, and I'd go to town, work the morning and he had a little dog named Jimmy he's take and walk in them hills all day, him and that little dog all by themselves, see, perfectly satisfied, wasn't worried about anything, but he was pretty good. One of the thing about it got a kick out of, see, I never made my bed, see, I'd come out there at night, I'd get in bed and a hornet would hit me, see, and I'd go sky high. He just laugh his head off, see. He get a kick out of that, see.

The tendency among educators would be to *correct* this speech segment in transcribing it, and thus make it fit the printed form. However, this eliminates rather than translates a great deal of meaning present in spoken words. Someone hearing this segment would find it both intelligible and effective communication. Our problem is to capture this *oral content* in a print mode.

Our education system offers little or no help to the student who wants to deal with the information conveyed by tone of voice. The nonverbal qualities of the voice lend shades of meaning that are typically lost in print. Two examples illustrate this point. How would you describe the speakers (age, sex, personality, etc.) of the following actual recorded statements?

> (A) He would walk a mile to make peace with somebody, you know . . . just like an uprising somewhere. He was always, if he got the word, he would always go and make peace for everybody . . . get everybody pleased on both sides. People at first . . . some of them would disagree, but in the end, he would win out. That's why I said if we had a President today

like Lincoln was, I don't think it would be all this excitement. I really don't.

(B) I like to earn money sort of. When anybody asks me to earn money, I accept it 'cause I like to get money. When I'm very low on money and somebody asks me if I should, and somebody asks me to do a commercial, I really accept it because I like to get money. And I'm not so money crazy, but it's just the fun of doing a commercial that I like about it.

There is relatively little information in the words of these statements that would tell you that (A) was a black woman in her seventies, and that (B) was a four-year-old boy. However, the vocal information present in a tape of these segments reveals these facts instantly. If you have a recorder you might try an experiment of recording friends, transcribing their words, and asking them a few weeks later if they can identify the person who made the transcribed statement. The information lost by putting spoken words on paper is often more important than the verbal content itself.

To some degree, tone of voice can be represented by type styles. What kinds of voices do the following suggest? Is there a typeface that communicates a harsh voice? Is there a typeface for young voices . . . nervous voices . . . angry voices? Can one typeface represent many voice qualities? Already, the problem is compounded, and we will have to explore other visual features of written words, e.g., page size, the presence or absence of illustrations, color, and spacing. For example, we do not have to print letters left-to-right and down the page in even rows. The following excerpt from a political speech illustrates how meaning changes as spacing is varied.

Two years ago I left the Superior Court to run for governor. At that time, I said I would be careful with the taxpayer's pocketbook, and I kept my word. I said I would improve the quality of government, and I kept my word. I said I would work in the best interests of both industry and labor, and I kept my word. I said

I would deal with drug abuse, and I kept my word. I said I would do more to control crime, and I kept my word. In all of these things, what I've said, I've done, and I kept my word. This, to me, is what being governor is all about.

Two years ago I left the Superior Court to run for governor. At that time,

> I said I would be careful with
> the taxpayer's pocketbook, and
> I kept my word.

> I said I would improve the quality
> of government, and I kept my word.

> I said I would work in the best
> interests of both industry and labor,
> and I kept my word.

> I said I would deal with drug abuse,
> and I kept my word.

> I said I would do more to control
> crime, and I kept my word.

In all of these things, what I've said, I've done, and I kept my word. This, to me, is what being governor is all about.

Two years ago I left the
Superior Court to run for
governor.

At that time, I said
I would be careful with
the taxpayer's pocketbook, and . . . . I kept my word.

I said I would improve
the quality of government, and . . . . I kept my word.

I said I would work
in the best interests of
both industry and labor, and . . . . I kept my word.

I said I would deal
with drug abuse, and. . . . . I kept my word.

I said I would do
more to control crime, and. . . . . I kept my word.

In all of these things,
what I've said, I've done, and . . . . I kept my word.

This, to me, is what being
governor is all about.

The design of type is a special skill of the typographer. However, since we are all affected by type, it should be studied and taught as part of a general curriculum.

TEACHING LISTENING

A wide range of *listening comprehension* programs claim to teach children, businessmen, and the average layman how to listen better. These programs are mislabeled. They should be

A child who is exposed to this form of typographic design . . .

. . . will reflect it in his own use of letters. But what would a teacher make of this?

called *oral reading comprehension,* because they teach listening the same way reading is taught. Typically, such programs contain two or three records with an actor reading aloud from a script. The listener is instructed to summarize what the actor says, or answer questions that test oral memory. They are concerned exclusively with the verbal content in oral messages. The listener is *not* asked, "Does the person speaking know what he is talking about?" "Do you believe what he says?" "In what situations would you pay attention to the speaker, and when would you ignore what he is saying?" or "What do you feel from the speaker?"

Listening comprehension programs teach people to *concentrate* on what is being said and remember each word. I find it difficult even to imagine someone listening to specific words and syllables, one by one, in a normal listening situation. We absorb and react to hundreds or thousands of auditory bits per second. A listener perceives a flow of information, and concentrates on a specific word only if it pops out of the context for some reason. The everyday listening experience is one of hearing whole sentences or complete utterances at a time. At a party, we may even listen to two or three conversations at once, sorting out those pieces of information we want to hear. We develop this acuity by growing up in the culture, and without the help (or constraint) of formal, institutionalized training. Further, we listen for *patterns* that relate new auditory information to stored experiences.

Listening programs, and classroom experiences generally, attempt to *unteach* the meaning children find in nonverbal sound patterns. In a test I conducted, a group of nursery school children were found to be 75 percent more accurate than their teachers in identifying nonverbal sounds. For example, the teachers could not distinguish between the sound of water being poured into a glass, and the sound of milk being poured into a glass. But this was easy for the students. The teachers were not only less skillful in making the distinction, they felt it was irrelevant. However, the same teachers could detect a subtle tone of reprimand in a principal's voice, a tone that students would not likely perceive.

These results can be explained, in part, by the training a teacher receives and, in turn, passes on to students. A teacher is conditioned to attend closely the verbal content in speech and to depend on a verbal label for nonspeech sounds in a formal classroom situation, while minimizing the rich communication in tone of voice and rhythms in nonspeech sounds. The children had not yet developed a dependence on verbal cues to identify sounds. And they had not yet been trained to minimize nonverbal speech communication.

Young people generally respond to intricate patterns of volume, rhythm, and pitch. This is due to the function served naturally by sound in early life—a function served (for many) by print in later life. The greatest amount of communication between mother and child is through nonverbal vocal cues. Children respond to the emotional quality and intonation of voices long before they understand the meaning of phonetic characteristics in voice. Tone of voice continues to play a vital communication role throughout life, but we are not trained to talk about it in the same way as verbal content. Indeed, people who are very sensitive to tone of voice often label their perception *intuition,* because they do not have a vocabulary for describing the vocal information they hear.

The problem educators encounter is not an inability of some students to *listen,* but their failure to *attend* what they hear. I believe we can best teach children to attend what they hear by getting them involved in communicating. If we can induce a student to ask questions, we will automatically produce a more attentive listener. He will be motivated to attend responses to *his* questions, and he will learn that information is acquired by becoming involved in the communication process. For some years, I have been teaching auditory perception to teen-agers. The first task I assign is an autobiography in sound. This encourages many students, for the first time in their lives, to ask other people how they feel about them. In response to such a

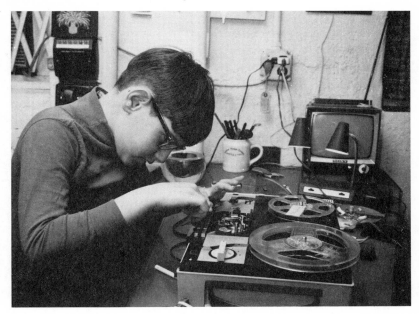

Editing of tapes can help develop more perceptive listening. One student commented, "Editing and splicing and going around asking questions, just working with sound, has made me listen a lot more."

question, one father told his daughter about the day she was born. In general, the material is much more personal than anything we ever hear on radio or television. The students become effective listeners because they are exposed to material that is worth hearing.

In addition, working with a tape recorder teaches a student the importance of *sound patterns* in communicating. Most sounds exist in a pattern with other sounds. One sound in the group may identify the entire pattern for a listener. A student may record the sound of a garbage truck, play it to the class, and find that no one understands it. However, if his recording contains the sound of a sanitationman banging a metal can against the back of the truck, listener perception will be higher.

A pattern of sounds that could have been a steam shovel, an electric generator, or a vacuum cleaner will become a garbage truck when one sound not common to any other pattern is heard. Similarly, a student from the suburbs may record an outdoor clothesline with numerous associative sounds (e.g., a window opening, someone asking for a shirt from a basket, etc.), and find that urban New York City students cannot identify it. Clotheslines have all but disappeared in mid-Manhattan. Lacking previous experience with a clothesline, the inner-city student cannot organize the various clothesline sounds into a meaningful pattern.

When a student is given the task of using sound to communicate, he must learn all the elements that affect his own listening. In coming to grips with this problem, he will become a more perceptive and attentive listener.

AUDIO-VISUAL AIDS IN THE CLASSROOM

Many education systems have recognized the need to develop multisensory perceptual skills. Audio-visual departments are common, and classroom use of films, records, and tapes is growing. However, the orientation of most educators who use audio-visual *aids* is still print-based. Even the word *aids* signals the implied subservience of electronic communication to print. This bias invariably affects classroom use of electronic equipment.

When I hear someone say he attended a multimedia show in school or that he received multimedia instruction, I think, "Oh, it must not have worked." It means that the audience was detached rather than involved, because they can separate the *form* of what they experienced from the thing itself. We do not refer to successful, integrated communication as *multimedia*. Television is multimedia, in the sense that it consists of auditory and visual stimuli. The same is true of film. But if a TV show or film is successful, we simply refer to it as *a good show* or *a good film,* never *a great multimedia show.* If an audience or class recognizes the communication as multimedia, it probably means that the program was a trick, a gimmick that did not integrate form and content. Whenever the technique stands out, the communication value is likely to be low.

In education, it is not sufficient to own audio-visual equipment. Its use must be patterned according to the perceptual and cognitive orientation of today's students. It must communicate meaning, not fill gaps in a teacher's schedule or aid print-based instruction. As long as the education establishment approaches communication from a print base, "multimedia" will remain a term for audio-visual materials that have little relevance or meaning to the student.

Perhaps the simplest way to reveal the delinquency of educators in the audio-visual area is to examine the quality of equipment that schools use to develop listening perception. A cartoon in the *New Yorker* showed a teacher with a phonograph on her desk, asking a student in the rear of the class, "And just why do you think Beethoven stinks, Johnny?" Well, Johnny thinks Beethoven or the Rolling Stones or the sound of a jet plane *stink* because she was playing them on a fifty-dollar phonograph, at low volume. Johnny meanwhile has a three-hundred-dollar stereo at home, and he plays material at its natural volume.

There is an absolute contradiction between the sound perception and media orientation children are developing at home and the perception fostered by the school environment. We would not think of using books in the classroom that have 60 percent less ink than ordinary books in the environment, but this is precisely what schools do in purchasing audio-visual equipment for classroom use. For example, the speakers in tape recorders and phonographs designed for school use are often two inches or four inches in size and powered by two-watt (or smaller) amplifiers. Speakers designed for home use are often ten or twelve inches in size and powered by forty-, fifty-, or one-hundred-watt amplifiers. In terms of quality, this is comparable to the difference between a poor-quality black-and-white photostat of a color picture, and the color picture itself.

Most educators do not know how to read equipment specification data and are therefore easy prey for manufacturers of inferior electronic hardware. The equipment specifications published by a manufacturer are usually accurate, but often they provide only specifications for unimportant features. I would not learn very much about a pair of pants if the manufacturer guaranteed that the material in the left leg was the same as the material in the right leg. Well, this is precisely what an electronics manufacturer is telling the school system when he states that his stereo has "matched speakers." Similarly, a specification sheet for a recorder may state, "Frequency response: plus or minus 4db, 50 cycles to 16,000 cycles." This is a measurement of what *can* be recorded on that machine. However, before this recorded sound reaches our ears it must pass through the speaker system on that recorder, and here the specifications may be quite different. Therefore, a potential buyer should know the specifications of sound coming from the speaker of a recorder. In the recorder cited above, the specifications for sound emanating from the speaker might read, "Frequency response: plus or minus 6db, 160 cycles to 7000 cycles." The difference in quality of sound between the two sets of specifications is equal to the difference between an excellent FM radio and a telephone.

Ironically, the same companies that make high-quality equipment for the general consumer market, make inferior equipment for the education market. One reason for this is the lack of understanding or concern on the part of manufacturers for how equipment will be used. Of equal importance, educators do not understand how audio-visual material should be used in the classroom, or what perceptual expectations a child brings to media experiences in the classroom. For example, although young people are the largest purchasers of two-channel auditory equipment and have oriented themselves to this form of listening, the education establishment does not use it at all. Most educators do not even know what it is.

The net effect of media delinquency by educators and our failure to research young people's perceptual habits is to increase the number of dropouts, both those who leave school physically, because they find it intolerable, and those who endure the classroom experience but drop out mentally, and thus fail to profit by it. It is not simply the case that education would be more effective if it spoke through the new technology. Rather, because our children learn the *language* of electronic technology before they enter school, we have no choice but to speak to them in their native tongue.

Sounds in the City

Thirty years ago it would have been impossible to imagine an apartment house with sealed windows. Today, it is common for new windows to be sealed and old windows to be closed, draped, and forgotten. It used to be of considerable importance whether windows were exposed to morning or afternoon sun. This affected lighting, temperature, and the *mood* of different rooms. Today, light and heat are controlled electronically, and if someone wants to affect the *mood* of an apartment, he usually tunes in a different radio station.

In the past, people were primarily influenced by sounds *of* the street—sounds generated by persons or objects on a block and carried through the air to the listener's ear. Today, we are primarily influenced by sounds that come *to* our street —sounds generated by persons or objects anywhere in the world and carried over radio waves or cables to the listener's ear.

In the past, an apartment was an urban dweller's window on the world. The apartment window extended his eyes and

ears to events on the street. Furthermore, the man who looked out his window thirty years ago perceived a unique world. No one else could witness exactly what he saw and heard. People on other blocks or in other cities could not see and hear the same events as he experienced them. Even a person at a nearby window would have a distinct and separate point of view. Sixteen people looking out sixteen windows might gain radically different perspectives on what was happening. A man and woman walking down the street might appear ordinary to fifteen people, but terrifying to the sixteenth—whose perspective allowed him to see a knife in the man's hand.

Thirty years ago streets were filled with activity. Vendors sold wares, children played, newsboys shouted headlines, and people sat on stoops talking. The man at a window determined the length of time he watched an event and the order of importance among activities on the street. He could choose to involve himself by going down to the street or even by shouting out the window. He rarely witnessed anything unexpected or beyond his ability to make sense of what he saw. A couple might be arguing loudly down the block, but he knew it was just Mr. Jones coming home from the neighborhood saloon and being confronted by his wife. Later, if he wished to tell someone what he saw, he could *not* assume that they had witnessed the same thing.

Today, the events that shape our lives are rarely observed through apartment windows. News, service, and life are no longer centered around the block. Sounds that seize our attention in day-to-day living are transmitted directly into our homes. And man's point of view in relation to this information has shifted radically. Whereas man once *perceived* sounds and sights of the street, now he *receives* electronically transmitted information. He is the screen on which information gathered by others is projected. With television, radio, and records—far from perceiving a unique world or enjoying a unique point of view—he shares the experience with millions. The visual and auditory perspective determined by camera

5

Outdoor advertising developed an awareness of walls as "a place to post signs."

and microphone placement is precisely the same for all viewers and listeners.

The shift in sources of information affecting our lives has turned the home inward and changed the meaning of *neighborhood*. Our common pool of media knowledge establishes a new set of neighbors for us, based not on geographic location but shared information. However, the new information environment *in which people live* coexists with the old city environment of streets and buildings where people are physically situated. This has created a number of problems.

NOISE POLLUTION

The present concern about noise pollution is based on a shift in the location of sounds we want to hear. We want to

As many of these billboards move to television, graffiti (or, poor people's advertising) replaces them.

hear sounds generated within our controlled electronic environment. Outdoor sounds therefore become noise, since they interfere with sounds coming into our homes via electronic media.

I have collected seventy-three articles on noise pollution. Without exception, all are concerned with outdoor sounds. A paragraph or two may decry teen-agers' music, and how it may cause deafness, but the main suggestion is that noise pollution originates outdoors. Yet there is no hard evidence that a typical urban street environment today is significantly louder than the typical street environment thirty years ago. If we have to contend with jet planes, air compressors, and more trucks, people living thirty years ago had more elevated subways, trolley cars on metal tracks, cobblestone roads, riveting on construction sites, and vendors shouting on the street. What has changed significantly is our center of interest. We are no longer con-

cerned about sounds coming from the street. We seal our windows, move to higher floors, and use radio, TV, and the telephone to stay in touch with a wider world. In addition, we
continuously play our radios or stereos to block out street
sounds that no longer provide information that will help us
in our daily living. Sound from the street was information in
the old environment. It is noise in the modern environment,
since it disturbs our relation to electronically mediated sounds
and information. We want to hear Dean Martin on TV, not a
would-be baritone walking home from a local pub.

Recognizing that street sounds have become *noise* because
of a shift in our interests does not eliminate the problem, but
it does provide a basis for dealing with it. A sound is not noise
because it is loud. It is noise because it disturbs us or interferes
with our activity. Noise is *unwanted sound.*

When the New York *Daily News'* Inquiring Photographer asked
people, "What unnecessary noise irritates you most?" he received
these replies:

The constant cackling of female voices in a social gathering.

The chiming of church bells next to my bedroom window at all
hours of the day and night.

Noise never bothers me. What can really bother me is silence,
deathly silence.

The noise that irritates me most is that made by a musician who
is slightly, ever so slightly, off key.

July 13, 1969

Some sounds are so loud they physically damage hearing, but
this is a small area in the over-all problem. Few people operate
air hammers or work next to jet planes. Antinoise advocates do
not always recognize this. Obviously, we should restrict sounds
that physically damage hearing. However, little attention has

been given to designing sounds that disturb less, even if volume cannot be reduced, or researching why certain sounds irritate more than others.

A student friend of mine once observed that the noisiest parties in his dormitory were the ones he was not invited to. Many sounds commonly labeled "noise" may become beautiful sounds in different contexts. For example, an infant's first scream, right after birth, is hardly *noise* to the mother. Nor is a fire engine's siren *noise* if it is speeding to put out a fire in *your* house, or a jet plane bringing home your son.

Time interacts with our judgment of noise. The longer a faucet drips, the noisier it becomes. The first ring of a doorbell tells you someone is at the door, but a second, third, and fourth ring in rapid succession, before you can reach the door, become noise.

Our activity at any given moment will strongly affect our judgment of sound as information or noise. On many occasions I have been in situations where my role as a recordist lessened my *judgment* of sound as noise and even my physiological reaction to it. Once I was standing directly under a helicopter as it landed. At first I reacted strongly to the tremendous volume of sound, but as I focused on the sound as a recording problem, my physiological reaction to the volume diminished.

Rather than simply measure decibel levels, those who design car horns, mufflers for air compressors, buses, jets, etc., should consider the character of the sound; how sound interacts with other sounds likely to be present; and the forms of social behavior most *polluted* by a given sound. In some cases we may even find that noise pollution can be reduced by *adding* sounds to the outdoor environment. Like positive odor conditioning with perfume, the addition of carefully designed sounds can interact with irritating sounds and produce pleasant, or at least acceptable, sounds. In Japan, for example, they play the sound of chirping birds over the public address system at railroad stations to help create a more tranquil environment.

A novel method of minimizing aircraft noise in homes near airports was outlined here yesterday at the monthly meeting of the Tri-State Transportation Commission.

J. Douglas Carroll Jr., the commission's executive director, reported that preliminary findings by acoustic experts showed that a low-level background hum inside a home allowed occupants "to operate more smoothly."

Insertion of such domestic background noises, he added, tended to improve the adaptability of people to aircraft noise as effectively as soundproofing buildings to keep out aviation noise.

Werner Bamberger
New York *Times*
January 9, 1972, p. 66

CRIME

In the late 1960s, Kitty Genovese was murdered on a major street in a heavily populated residential area. It was not a quick

If you're ever attacked in a hallway, don't yell "Help," yell "Fire."
New York City policeman
Personal interview

death. She fought her attacker for several minutes, all the while screaming for help. No one came to her assistance or even called the police. Yet an investigation following the murder revealed that thirty-seven people heard her screams.

Editorials decried the cowardice and callousness of those thirty-seven, and called for more police protection. The outcries were justified, but no editorials really explored the problem. *Cowardice* might explain why no one went down to the street to help her. But why did no one call the police? *Callous-*

ness might be a satisfactory answer for one or two people not calling—but not thirty-seven.

If we view the circumstances surrounding the Genovese murder as a communication problem, it becomes important that all thirty-seven who heard her were inside a building, while she was outside. People inside a city building tend to reject information from outside that closed space. They are conditioned to respond to sound generated internally. Sound from outside is usually noise, unwanted sound, interfering with inside activity.

Our personal world is defined by the communications network that provides important information for life functions. More and more, this network involves electronically mediated communication centered within our apartment space. Distant events, mediated through radio and television, are personally experienced inside our living rooms. They move us emotionally and help us relate to others who have witnessed the same events. The street in front of our apartment, however, is not part of this electronically mediated world. We live in a global village which, like the tribal village, is surrounded by a dangerous no-man's-land: our streets.

Kitty Genovese may have been the first startling, terrifying example of just how isolated the street has become. When an apartment dweller leaves his house he loses touch with his *world*. He is alone, even on a crowded street. The space between our central electronic environment (the home) and various mini-electronic environments such as a car or office building, is isolated from the new community.

On subways, for example, we are in an enclosed space but we are not in contact with our *world*. Further, we are trapped with foreign bodies. We attempt to deal with this hostile environment by not talking to anyone and hoping no one will talk to us. If someone speaks to us, we suspect he is drunk, neurotic, an addict, or a mugger. We dare not look at another person, and suspect anyone who looks at us. We stare at a door or the floor, at advertising above the seats, or an unoccupied part of the train, or hold paper in front of our face to minimize the chance of eye contact with another person. It is not uncommon on a New York subway to find a person who is mentally deranged, carrying on a loud conversation with himself. As long as he does not address himself to anyone in particular, and as long as he doesn't touch or stare at anyone, no one is alarmed. In this environment, a future Kitty Genovese is not likely to find many people coming to her aid. The same person who angrily calls the network's switchboard if a football game is interrupted, or telegraphs a message of protest to the FCC if Johnny Carson tells a slightly off-color joke may not respond to a shout for help in the subway because it takes place in an environment where verbal communication is typically hostile.

In many cities, the sounds of a bottle breaking, a garbage can being overturned and the lid rolling onto the street, and men shouting and cursing are very familiar. Since we are not involved in the street community, we cannot identify the sound with a given individual or place it in a more complete context. If we cannot identify the sound as an element in a larger behavioral pattern, it is likely to become impersonalized for us. The nightly barrage of impersonal sounds on city streets is like salty air for the fisherman; it becomes part of our unconscious environment.

Some Applications

CABLE AND CASSETTES

A college student I know tells me that he can break off a relationship with one girl, begin dating a new girl, and it will seem like a continuation, not a change. He can develop a conversation with the first girl and continue it with the second as if he were still speaking to the first girl. By the same token, he performs a boyfriend role for them. He is just like everyone else they have dated.

This would probably not have been possible before radio. Our shared experiences with electronic communications have produced a common knowledge of events and a common understanding of the world. We share a collective consciousness and a synchronous relation to each other, hence Marshall McLuhan and Edmund Carpenter's designation of our society as *tribal*. All members of a university community behave synchronously. And on a larger scale, the university environment is in sync with all other environments that share the same media inputs.

The development of cable networks and the widespread use of various cassette systems may blow our tribal culture apart, creating a new set of *special interest* mass audiences. Cable will also permit two-way communication. This will create feedback by the public, which may disrupt the single-minded knowledge of world events fostered by the present communication structure. And once cassette systems become widely used, people will receive information on a more decentralized basis. This opens up the possibility of re-establishing autonomous local communities and creating a new form of individualism. Also, it will mark the end of our global village as the dominant environment.

In the near future, the effects of the new technology are not likely to be strongly felt because of the way it will be used. The hardware manufacturers of the new systems are utilizing the previous communications systems' software producers. This is like a marriage between the undertaker and the corpse. Cable and cassettes are about to embalm and bury network television and the Hollywood film distribution system, but they are marrying these old environments for investment purposes. RCA, McGraw-Hill, and CBS are among the largest investors in cable and cassettes. As a result, we will have to struggle through "I Love Lucy" cassettes and all-movie channels on our cable before new programming will emerge.

MNEMONIC SPEECH

In preliterate Western societies, important historical events, social customs, religious beliefs, etc., were retained through a variety of auditory, mnemonic structures. All preserved communication was orally shaped in the form of epic poetry, ballads, limericks, etc. These auditory, mnemonic structures were a frame of reference for all members of the speech community. They served not only as learning or memory aids, but as enjoyable group activity in which response to an epic poet or

ballad singer produced hypnotic communal experiences. Eric
Havelock describes the phenomenon in Homeric Greece:

> You did not learn your ethics, politics, skills and directives, by
> having them presented to you as a corpus for silent study, re-
> flection and absorption. You were not asked to grasp their prin-
> ciples through rational analysis. You were not invited to so
> much as think of them. Instead you submitted to the paideutic
> spell. You allowed yourself to become musical in the functional
> sense of that Greek term.
>
> *Preface to Plato*
> Grosset & Dunlap
> New York, 1963, p. 159

With the spread of literacy and the mechanization of printing,
the oral shape of mnemonic devices gave way to print-based
memory, which remained the principle means of retaining information for the next five hundred years. Learning mecha-
nisms based on memory were first challenged in this century
with the development of radio technology. Here was a chance
for auditory communication to reassert itself. But when radio
came along, the broadcasting community did not ask itself:
"Now that we are dealing with the spoken word again, what
are the principles by which it is structured, and how does it
function in people's lives?" They simply applied their print
orientation to radio programming. All copy was written and
read according to the rules of grammar—though grammar is
a set of rules for putting words on paper, not for communicating orally in social contexts. The first auditory-based mnemonic
device to break into radio was the jingle, which employed
simple rhyme to aid listener retention of a simplistic message. Ever since the first notes for Interwoven Socks, reputed
to be the first singing commercial, were sung by Billy Jones
and Ernie Hare, the Happiness Boys, the jingle established
itself as a dominant technique in radio commercials. I compare the jingle to a nose cold: You pick it up in the environment, it's infectious, contagious, hard to lose, and embarrassing

(it keeps on running). But it does not communicate meaning. It is a structure that catches everyone for a while, but in a short time it is gone—with no lasting effect. In a commercial song or jingle, the sounds of words are taken out of their natural communication context and manipulated to fit the rhythm of the jingle. This can aid a listener's *retention* of the words, but it does not attach the words to actual situations (where those words are heard in a different rhythmic pattern). In a jingle, words lose the meaning conveyed by the rhythm in a real speech situation. This is a devastating loss, since *spoken words do not have a meaning isolated from their rhythm.*

The development of auditory-based mnemonic aids, other than the jingle, has not received much attention. Two announcers, Bob Landers and Bob Marcato, have developed speaking styles that structure words as natural speech sounds, rather than employ written grammatical structure as a frame of reference. And in my early work, I attempted to record and design sounds that communicated auditory meanings unto themselves rather than act as decorations (or sound effects) for verbal cues. More recently, I have explored several areas, e.g., the structure of rock music, two-channel listening, and phonemic restoration, and have developed a way of designing speech to aid retention without altering natural speech rhythms. I call it *mnemonic speech.*

Mnemonic speech design builds on several cornerstones. First, the recent work on phonemic restoration has demonstrated that the brain can fill in and *hear* phonemes not actually present in speech. In other words, if I record a sentence such as, "The state governors met with their respective legislatures convening in the capital city," cut out the "gisla" in "le*gisla*tures," and substitute a cough or some extraneous sound, a listener will *hear* the entire word when it is played in a proper context. He will hear both the complete word "legislatures" and the cough sound, even though the "gisla" in "le*gisla*tures" is not physically present. A question then arises, can we substitute phonemes from other words for the phoneme extracted from the original word, and still retain meaning in both words? And what about the loss of linear continuity if words overlap each other? Well, a second cornerstone of mnemonic speech rests on the auditory structures developed in rock music. The voice overlays in rock music are structurally similar to those in mnemonic speech, though in rock music the overlays usually involve two different voices or one singer playing two distinct roles (e.g., lead singer and background accompaniment), so a listener has the added help of separate voice characteristics. I was interested in multiple phonemic overlays for a single speaker, as well as two or three separate speakers. Single-speaker phonemic overlays do not exist in real life. Our voice cannot produce two phonemes simultaneously. In order to render a mnemonic speech design perceptible to a listener, one has to create new phonemic relationships that both retain the natural rhythms of words and build on structural patterns experienced by the listener in other forms, such as music.

Briefly, mnemonic speech is a way of designing materials to build rhythmic patterns not obvious but inherent in the original material, while retaining the essential speech rhythms that give meaning to the words. The editing procedure involves cutting the original tape into segments, in A-B fashion (just like film), and placing them on separate recorders. On the A tape, blank leader tape fills in the spaces where sound is present on the B track, and vice versa for the B tape. The leader does not fill in all the space, however. By using less leader tape than is required to match the sound on the opposite track, overlays will occur at those points where sound is present on both tracks. The A and B tracks are placed on separate recorders and fed into a third recorder, producing the overlays. Of course, this model is an oversimplified one. The actual design involves a rather complex interaction of overlays and cutting certain parts of the tape.

In a given speech segment, certain pauses and stress patterns are necessary to communicate the meaning intended by the speaker. For example, *"big* house" does not indicate the same thing as "big *house"* or *"big-house."* The first indicates a house that is big; the second, a big *house* as opposed to a big *bridge* or a big *tree;* the third, a prison. However, many pauses and stress features are not so important. These can be redesigned and overlapped to create new rhythms. Similarly, in a given context we can recognize many words from one or two phonemes. For example, if I say, "By 1976, there'll be safer bumpers on all automo . . ." you don't need "biles" to understand the sentence. A listener can fill this in. These unnecessary phonemes may also be redesigned to create new patterns. As you may have noticed, this design technique also compresses time. Often, the mnemonic version is one half the time of the original recording, and in one case, a forty-second speech segment was reduced to ten seconds.

Mnemonic speech has been quite successful thus far, though it has only been applied in a few areas. There is a great opportunity here for breaking speech away from its linear shackles and making it a distinct auditory form again. Indeed, this is the third cornerstone of mnemonic speech: It fulfills many of the requirements for *auditory*-based mnemonic aids. It is

ON LANGUAGE IN TRIBAL SOCIETIES

Language is a storage system for the collective experience of the tribe. Every time a speaker plays back that language, he releases a whole charge of ancient perceptions and memories. This involves him in the reality of the whole tribe. Language is a kind of corporate dream: it involves every member of the tribe all of the time in a great echo chamber.

Ted Carpenter
They Became What They Beheld
Outerbridge & Dienstfrey
New York, 1970

an *original* form of hearing for records, radio, or TV, not just a *copy* of another environment. It is also a popular form. A listener finds the rhythms created much like rock music rhythms. It demands audience participation. Since many of the sounds are not present on the tape, they only become real in the listener's mind, as he fills in the missing phonemes. Furthermore, the effect of mnemonic speech varies with the contextual associations a listener brings to the event. It is not a vehicle for teaching a listener distinctly new information. Rather, it tunes into his experiences, resonates with them, and reorganizes the meaning of those experiences. For example, in a commercial for the movie *Woodstock*, I designed the names of the rock groups in the movie into mnemonic speech. For many adults, the names were imperceptible, because the full names were not sufficiently isolated for them to hear and *learn*. For teen-agers, or those who knew the rock groups' names, the design was both pleasant to the ear and clearly perceptible. They recognized the names of their favorite groups and tuned in the names they wanted to hear. Another commercial, for a bank, produced exactly the opposite result. Here, a list of bank services was compressed even more than the rock groups' names (the bank spot compressed forty seconds into ten, while the rock spot compressed twenty-four seconds into eight). Adults had no difficulty perceiving all the services mentioned, but teen-agers, who have less familiarity with banking, could perceive only some of the items mentioned. Teen-agers who heard both spots felt certain that the banking spot was more compressed. Adults judged the relative compression of the two spots exactly opposite.

THE RECORDING STUDIO

Shortly after he developed a technique for capturing sound, Thomas Edison built what he thought was the perfect recording instrument. It had a solid brass horn 135 feet long, 5 feet in diameter at the point of sound input, and tapering to 1 inch at the point where it attached to the wax cylinder recorder.

With a recording horn like Edison's, extraneous sounds in the immediate environment had to be minimized or eliminated. This created the need for a studio environment to keep out unwanted sounds. Recording studios were thus designed for silence, not sound. They were controlled environments, unlike the real world. Within the studio, sound had to be manipulated to create a symbolic representation of reality. People accepted and believed these sounds because they learned to accept and believe conventions observed by those who created communications. These *rules,* which governed recordings in studios for many years, throw a good deal of light on the problem of rendering sound that is *believable* for the listening audience.

In everyday listening experiences, we expect sound in an outdoor setting to be relatively *dead* (i.e., it has little reverberation, since there are few surfaces nearby that might reflect the sound), and sound in an indoor setting to vary in degrees of *liveness* (e.g., bathrooms have a great deal of reverberation; living rooms, a lesser amount). However, studios consistently reverse the real-life expectation of outdoor sound in post-dubbing a film. They will artificially add reverberation to a studio recording to render it *outdoor sound.* The rule so pervaded Hollywood that they would add reverberation to a recording actually made outdoors—so it would sound like the outdoor sounds created artificially in studios.

Once cases and handles were put on recorders, the studio became obsolete. The *world* should have become our recording studio, and the buildings we called studios should have become workshops where sound could be edited and mixed. Only a few people have understood this and used real-life environments to create sound communication. *Reality* sound recording is inherently more believable than symbolic representation of reality, because it communicates sounds that people have heard before in their lives. The context in which we have experienced previous auditory information, both the acoustic environment and the people interacting with us in that context, are just as much a part of the event as the physical sound waves we received and labeled *communication*. If someone wishes to heighten the believability of sound, he must understand the history of our experience with similar sounds and the various contexts in which these sounds became meaningful.

It is not surprising that only a very small percentage of the population has ever been in a radio station or a recording studio. Yet 99 percent of the narrators and actors we hear on radio or TV are recorded in studios. The conventions that arose out of technological limitations in old radio and film sound have been thoughtlessly perpetuated in the new sound environment. Our perception of these sounds cannot benefit from the rich contextual associations evoked by sounds recorded in a context we've experienced in our lives. Thus an actor recorded in an *everyday life* location is more believable than the same actor, with the same lines, recorded in a studio. If the listener can relate the environment in which the recording is made to his own experience of similar environments, the believability of the recording will be increased. Also, with the improvements in electronic equipment (both recording equipment and playback units in the home), we can now hear the studio environment where the recording is made. If you listen to FM radio with headphones, it is easy to perceive the kind of room in which the announcer is speaking. In this situation, the unreal studio environment is perceived as more unrelated to our lives than ever before. Conversely, recordings made in real environments communicate more information than ever before.

With today's multichannel sound communication, particularly in rock music, our relation to electronically mediated auditory information is shifting from environmental re-creation to environmental recreation. That is, the ideal of creating

sound in a person's living room that is exactly like the sound
he would hear were he at a concert (environmental re-creation) is less relevant. Much of rock music is never performed
anywhere. It is constructed, layer by layer, over time, on multi-
track recorders. The record or tape is the original piece of
music. It is not a copy of a performance. The way you use the
record in your home (volume setting, speaker placement,
etc.) is the performance (environmental recreation). In this
new relation to sound, the contextual associations we bring
to the listening event are our past experiences of similar electronically mediated auditory forms. The sound studio, in this
context, once again becomes relevant. However, its function is
totally different from Edison's brass horn or the Hollywood
sound stage. The studio today creates packages of sound that
will be brought to the home for environmental recreation. Since
the piece of communication will be used in such a new way
(e.g., one girl described a record as "that kind of sound where
you can sandwich your head between two speakers and take
off"), the sound designer must bring to the studio a thorough
knowledge of how his sound will function in people's lives,
and how their reception of sound will interact with previous
experiences of other electronically mediated information. We
are now capable of taking listeners on outer trips to other
environments or inner trips in which a person's mind is turned
inward and resonates with our stimuli.

FREUD AND THE ESKIMOS

Just as the print mode, prior to the development of electronics, encouraged a linear patterning of all communication,
electronic media patterning now dominates our communication environment. As a result, we find many forms of social
behavior with a parallel structure to electronic media.

The rise of behaviorist therapy and the decline of Freudian
psychoanalysis parallels the increasing use of electronic media

as environmental surround. Freud's writing emerged from a print-based psychological backdrop. His theories cannot function with auditory-based tribal cultures, of the old or new variety. Freud could never cure an Eskimo, and he would be confounded by the average teen-ager today. A Freudian approach analyzes someone's personal, psychological *history*. This has little meaning for a person living in a succession of current, fleeting moments. Freudians view the present as a product of the past. They attempt to relate childhood experiences to problems in later life, rather than carefully observing how individuals function in the present. Behaviorist therapy, based on conditioning and instantaneous feedback, which create attachments between stimuli and responses, is more in tune with our culture's psychological problems. Psychiatrists find that the predominant mental health problem today is impulse control. As Allen Bergin notes,

> Many clinicians know that increasing numbers of clients are seeking treatment for problems of impulse control, such as aggression and violence, sexual excesses and perversions, alcoholism, drug addiction, and garden variety difficulties, e.g., overeating and smoking.

People with impulse control problems respond instantly, and incorrectly, to a stimulus in their environment. The rise of such problems parallels our increasing involvement with electronic media.

Similarly, much sociological research today centers on cultural phenomena arising from an orientation toward the current fleeting moment and the values of the *now* generation. It is more than curious that a society in which impulse control is a major problem, and interest in the current fleeting moment in time is at a peak, also receives most of its information in the form of fleeting sound vibrations on radio and fleeting light impulses on television. The reality that is communicated to us only exists for an instantaneous second in a speaker's horn or on a picture tube. The world is thus electronically fractured, recorded, transmitted, received, and reassembled in the human brain. The *now* generation is thus a product of the *now* quality of perception.

~~~~~~

I put this book together during the period between 1970 and 1973. It reflects my thinking as of the date I am writing this postscript. However, you are likely reading these words many months (or even years) after they were put to paper. I therefore caution you to interpret these thoughts in the context of your own communication environment.

The specific applications of the resonance principle are totally dependent on the context where communication takes place. For this reason, I have tried to talk more about how one can use the resonance principle in dealing with communication problems, rather than spell out a formula for creating communications. There are no permanent formulas. As you read these words, video cartridges, extended dynamic range, sound-oriented TV, or some other technological advance may have changed the communication context that gives meaning to your messages or stimuli. The resonance principle suggests that the starting point for understanding and creating

communication lies in examining the communication environment you are living in at this moment, and the context within
which any stimuli you create will be received.

Tony Schwartz

March 18, 1973

Index

Acoustic (auditory) base, 6ff. (*see also* Auditory communication; Environment, electronic; specific aspects); of electronic media, 11–18, 26–40, 41ff.; linear communication and, 6–11; patterning of stored auditory experiences and, 27–40, 41ff.; speech and writing and, 118–27

Acoustic setting (acoustic environment), 29–40, 41ff. (*see also* Acoustic [auditory] base; Environment, electronic; specific aspects, kinds); speech and writing and, 118–27

Advertising, 56–79 (*see also* Advertising agencies; specific aspects, kinds, media); commercials and (*see* Commercials); consumerism and consumers and, 77–79 (*see also* Consumerism; Consumers); creating stimuli and, 54–55; designing commercials and, 72–74; and media environment for commercials, 74–77; outdoor, 140, 141; and political campaigns, 80–107; recall and associations and, 69–72; research and, 67–69, 100–5; and resonance in political advertising, 92–100; and truth, 20–22

Advertising agencies (*see also* Advertising): and advertising research, 67–69, 100–5; and time buying, 104–5; and truth in advertising, 20–22

Advertising research, 67–69, 100–5

Aircraft noise, minimizing of, 144, 145

Alioto (Joseph L.) mayoralty campaign (1971), 91

Amateur radio, xii

Ambient sound level, 27ff., 41ff.

American Cancer Society, 55

Amplification of sound, 47–50. *See also* Sound; Volume of sound

Anderson, Jack, 98

Anderson, Margaret B., quoted on Robert Frost and speech, 120, 123

Antismoking campaign, message creation and, 55